UNIVERSITIES
AND THE MYTH
OF CULTURAL
DECLINE

UNIVERSITIES

AND

THE MYTH

OF CULTURAL

DECLINE

Jerry Herron

Wayne State University Press
Detroit 1988

Library of Congress Cataloging in Publication Data
Herron, Jerry, 1949–
    Universities and the myth of cultural decline / Jerry Herron.
        p.   cm.
    Bibliography: p.
    ISBN 0-8143-2068-6 (alk. paper). ISBN 0-8143-2069-4 (pbk. : alk.
paper)
    1. Educational anthropology—United States. 2. Education, Higher—
United States. 3. Education, Humanistic—United States.
I. Title.
LB45.H47 1988
378'.012—dc19   88-10081
                                                                          CIP

Jerry Herron is Assistant Professor of English at Wayne
State University. Dr. Herron received his M.A. and his
Ph.D. from Indiana University. He edited two volumes of
W. D. Howells: Selected Letters. Dr. Herron has written
reviews and articles on popular culture and on literature
for *Criticism, Journal of American Culture, Social Text,
New England Quarterly*, and *Antioch Review*.

The Manuscript was edited by Robert S. Demorest. The
cover was designed by Jim Billingsley. The typeface for
the text and the display is Times Roman. The book is
printed on 55-lb. Glatfelter text paper. The cloth edition is
bound in Holliston Mills' Roxite Linen.

Manufactured in the United States of America.

Today, how can we not speak of the university?

—Jacques Derrida

We act in order to justify the acts which we have already committed. We take steps whose only function is to give meaning to the steps we have already taken. Obstinately, we stay on at the bad hotel in order to give meaning to the fact that we were once stupid enough to check in there.

—Lars Gustafsson

Contents

Foreword   9

Acknowledgments   21

Introduction   23

1. Crisis   33

2. Work   43

3. History   63

4. Language   75

5. Teachers and Students   93

6. Subjects   117

   Conclusion   131

   Appendix   137

   Notes   139

Foreword

Cardinal Newman got his way. Newman's conception of liberal education in *The Idea of a University* assumed that intellectual culture should exist not primarily to serve utilitarian ends but to be an end in itself. Jerry Herron argues that Newman's vision of culture as an end in itself has been all too thoroughly fulfilled in the present state of humanities education, though hardly in the way Newman intended. The humanities *have* become ends in themselves, but only because they have no other end, because they have lost their social function.

As Herron puts it, "Newman wanted liberal education to be special, to be set apart. Now it surely is that." In a society which classifies intellectual culture under the Sunday-supplement category "Arts and Leisure," there is no need to worry about culture becoming subordinated to instrumental ends. It is not thought to have any.

So stated, Herron's argument may sound like yet another version of that very "myth of cultural decline" that Herron is attempting to lay to rest. Herron certainly does present the academic humanities as an institution in deep trouble, yet the aim of his book is to provide a constructive alternative to the nostalgia and pessimism now being promoted with great popular success by numerous hand-wringers and viewers-with-alarm. In the first place, for Herron what contemporary academic humanists do is neither decadent or nihilistic, as the hand-wringers so often charge. In the second place, for Herron humanistic culture of the universities is not *really* irrelevant to modern society; it has only made itself *look* as if it is by being more incoherent as an institution than it needs to be. The problem of the humanities, as Herron sees it, lies neither in the social irrelevance of its concerns nor the nihilism and relativism of its practitioners but in a larger structural problem which he describes as a problem of "symbolic representation."

In short, Herron argues that the humanities have ceased to stand for anything coherent or useful in the eyes of their constituents. But for him the explanation is not that humanists have sold out to politics or deconstruction or even that they have buried themselves in unintelligible jargon. It is that the intellectual and political conversation that humanists represent is only latent, rather than publicly manifest. This is where the misleading belief that the humanities should be taught for their own sake comes in, for as long as humanists accept a mistaken account of their actual relation (or in this case their non-relation) to their society they figure to have trouble making their real relation clear to outsiders.

Herron is here pointing out a paradox that seems to have escaped notice: that the great success of humanistic culture in the modern university has derived from the very social usefulness that its official defenders have usually denied or minimized. When Newman and other Victorian sages were promoting humanistic culture as a form of disinterested knowledge for its own sake, that culture was functioning as a powerful instrument in the shaping of middle class consciousness and the legitimation of middle class mobility. Of course, this was the problem—the vulgar utility of culture as a means of upward mobility had to be disguised in order to make that mobility seem less vulgar. Nevertheless, when the middle classes came to power in England and America in the nineteenth century, classical humanistic education continued to be a prerequisite to the professions and to positions of national leadership. In other words, the humanities owe their inherited educational and social prestige to the fact that they have *not* existed in a disinterested realm, but have directly contributed to the middle class world of work and success.

But today, humanistic culture is not only no longer so obviously a prerequisite for advancing up the vocational ladder, it is no longer clearly needed as a means of legitimating social success. The culture of many of our most spectacularly successful citizens (think, for example, of the careers of the Hon. Richard J. Daley, Richard Nixon, and Ronald Reagan) is not the humanistic culture of Newman and Arnold, but the mass culture of movies, television, and sports. The literacy that now tends to accompany American success is the type that Herron, borrowing a term from Enzensberger, calls "second order illiteracy," which is another way of saying that being successful depends on *not* acquiring the humanistic culture of Newman and Arnold.

Herron's point is that in such a situation, where the social function of the academic humanities has come into question, trying to rebuild those humanities upon the liberal rationale of culture for its own sake can only deepen their plight. If the humanities have never really functioned purely for their own sake, we cannot revitalize them by trying to make them function that way now. Herron says, in effect, let's face it: the humanities can be justified in a world of work and power only by proving useful in the world of work and power, though not necessarily simply by being put in the service of the already powerful. For Herron this means frankly recognizing that intellectual culture and the humanities too are a form of *work* and can serve a social function only insofar as they are instrumental to the world of work.

What keeps this argument from being merely a plea for making the humanities an adjunct to technocratic capitalism is Herron's very broad conception of "work." For Herron, "work" includes everything from the kind of jobs humanities students may hope to get in businesses and corporations to the sometimes esoteric analyses which culture critics devise to understand and change the world. In other words, for Herron it is important that we stop viewing the work of "intellectuals" as fundamentally different and less useful than other forms of work. At one point, he suggests that just as, at the end of the nineteenth century, the model of the humanist underwent an evolution from the gentleman amateur to the professional scholar, it now needs to undergo a further evolution from the scholar to the cultural intellectual. That some such evolution may in fact be taking place is suggested by the recent advent in universities of a new generation of young academic cultural intellectuals like Herron himself. (In some ways, this is very Arnoldian. In fairness to Newman and Arnold, it was the critical work of the general intellectual that was the *real* utilitarian function of culture for them, whatever they may have said about culture for its own sake.)

Herron's point is that the concerns of such general intellectuals could give the university humanities the coherence they now sorely lack. The university has the potential of becoming an intellectual community but has never managed to be one. The academic humanities harbor a general intellectual conversation that could potentially be interesting and even useful to society at large, but it is a conversation that the humanities have not been able to make visible and available in coherent form.

What makes Herron's outlook refreshing, seen against the background of current educational discussion, is that it starts from the frank recognition—always dismissed with contempt by conservatives—that the university has always served an *ideological* function in our society. As Herron puts it, the university has offered "*potential* access to the instruments of privilege and control" and extended "the ultimate promise of individualist democracy that you can make whatever you want of yourself. . . . Even for the 'educated classes,' knowledge rarely served as its own end, despite what Cardinal Newman may have thought. On the contrary, knowledge—culture—remained desirable because it got you around in the world."

Of course the way humanistic culture "got you around in the world" was to associate you with a class of gentlemen who presumably cared more for leisure than for getting around in the world. The most useful thing about culture was the appearance of graceful uselessness it conferred on those suspected of being all too crudely useful. The secret of culture was that it was effective in the world without seeming to be too vulgarly so:

> the most important feature of Arnold's university is that it worked. The language of "culture" was immediately (however self-consciously) practical. It accomplished a crucial task for the middle class who found themselves in need of an idiom, an ideology with which to economize their social and political identity, and with which to remove from that identity—as from their money—the taint of having been recently "made." The university worked because it taught people who went there—or who participated vicariously in its social forms—how to represent their relations both to each other and to the conditions responsible for their arrival "in the world." It lent them the weight of a cultural tradition by which the "individual" might escape the irrelevance of recent creation.

Here is a good example of the way Herron treats the university as a problem of "symbolic representation." Adapting a term from recent semiotic and hermeneutic theorizing, he argues that the university humanities have lost the "representational" function they served when their acquisition was a touchstone of class status and mobility. The problem is that the university "doesn't even attempt to address itself to the question of what its representations stand for, except as an invocation of powerless cultural myths," such as the myth that the university stands for unified cultural tradition—or at least did so back in the good old days before all the relativists and nihilists descended on us.

The problem with the conservative theory of humanistic decline (apart from being historically misinformed and false) is that once it is accepted, the only practical options become either ritualistic nostalgia or coercive imposition of a traditional conception of culture resisted by many Americans. Conservatives always cry foul when the specter of authoritarianism and elitism is raised against them, but they never bother to think through the problems posed for education in a democratic society, one which is committed to respecting a variety of competing conceptions of tradition, culture, and standards. It is difficult to see how else a traditionalist conception of culture could be superimposed on a society of dissonant and contentious groups except by coercive or authoritarian means.

Such, in very schematic outline, is what I take to be the argument of Herron's challenging book. (Though I may have Graffianized Herron in the process of summarizing him—or perhaps Graff has been Herronized—it should not matter.) There are some ambiguities in this argument, which I think Herron wisely leaves intact, although he might have confronted them more directly than he does. It is liberating to take the humanities down from the pedestal of "culture" and reunite them with the world of "work," and it is healthy to remind us that cultural analysis and interpretation are as much a form of work as any. But how precisely is the work of cultural intellectuals to be integrated with the work of engineers and businessmen? Do we really know how vocationally useful the culture of the humanities is or can be? As long as that culture is as incoherent as Herron shows it to be, isn't it hard to tell?

To put the same kind of question another way, if the work which the humanities exemplify includes both the work of corporate America and the work of radical intellectual critics of corporate America, then are the humanities cultural or countercultural? It is interesting to look at the way the official publicity of humanities departments tends to hedge on this question. English departments, for example, characteristically tell students that if they major in English they will learn to become independent thinkers who will fearlessly question the established beliefs and institutions of their society—but that, additionally, they will acquire the skills that will qualify them for the professions. If you study English, you will learn how to see through corporate capitalism while qualifying for a job at IBM!

The contradiction between the cultural and countercultural ideals of humanistic education is a glaring one, but it is one that is imbedded in American society as a whole and the academic humanities merely reflect it. For the time being, anyway, it is fair to assume that this contradiction is not going to be resolved, but then it would not have to be resolved in order for educational institutions to make something productive out of it. That is, it would be useful if the contradiction between the cultural and countercultural aspects of the humanities could be brought out into the open and made part of the context in which students study the humanities and make sense of their lives. Since Herron wants the humanities to recognize, and begin to make themselves *about*, their own ideological contradictions, he might have started with the contradictions in that concept of work that is so central to his analysis.

In arguing that the university has ceased to "stand for" anything, Herron's diagnosis is not too far from that of current conservatives (in fact his use of the term "representation" derives as much from the conservative tradition as from recent semiotic theory). But as I have already suggested, Herron differs crucially from the conservatives in recognizing that the university has represented no single, unitary tradition, or that when it has this was only because it was constituted undemocratically and excluded dissenting traditions. Recent demographic change underlies the current flap over whether and how the Great Books are being taught and the status of "theory." What really makes the anti-theory traditionalists so angry is that educational definitions, issues, and decisions that they for so long had the power to determine as a matter of course now have to be defended by argument—and against a whole array of new groups that previously had no say in the matter. For the traditionalists, this new situation is "relativism," but an older word for it would be "democracy."

Herron, by contrast, argues that, in a democratic society, for the university to stand for a coherent culture has to mean standing for a culture of conflict and debate rather than a culture of homogeneous values and beliefs, which could only be imposed by undemocratic means. Herron can therefore agree with secretary of education William Bennett that in the University today "we don't know what we're doing," but without agreeing that "the dead coherence of culture" as embodied in Bennett's frozen list of decontextualized texts "offers a viable solution." Or again, Herron can echo Bennett in complaining that "we never think or talk about who is being taught, about the kind of individual we collectively stand for," but without Bennett's implication that there is some one "kind of individual" universities should produce. Or again, Herron can echo the conservative objection that "discussions of curriculum always end up a subject-less proxy fight in behalf of vested interest," but without the conservative hypocrisy that declares it is only the Left that has vested interests, that the conservative conception of curriculum is disinterested and above politics and ideology.

What differentiates Herron's view from that of the cultural right is that instead of seeking to *protect* the curriculum from the contamination of ideological conflict, Herron would have the curriculum frankly stage the confrontation of ideological conflict and *exploit* its untapped educational potential. He would have university faculties bring their conflicting ideologies into open engagement instead of harboring them in separation and hiding the clashes from students. For it is only by bringing conflicts of ideology out into the open that observers and participants can discover what is at stake in them, can see their representational meaning. Instead of the "pseudo-coherence," as Herron terms it, of E. D. Hirsch's dreary cultural literacy lists or Allan Bloom's Platonic Ideas, Herron would base educational coherence on "the confrontations on which any institutional literacy is founded," namely the real-life conflicts of the culture, as understood and formulated by the intellectual disciplines and their critics.

On the other hand, Herron recognizes, as other recent critics on the left have not always recognized, that to say that the university has an ideological function is only to begin a discussion, not to end it. Though "ideology" is one of his favorite words, Herron avoids any reductive account of what the ideology of the university today *is*, and he does not write in the familiar current tone of Lefter-than-Thou superiority. In one place, Herron amusingly and pointedly recounts his efforts to teach Michel Foucault's *Discipline and Punish* to prison inmates, pointing out to them how both they and he were " 'written,' as subjects of state surveillance." The trouble was, as Herron quickly learned, that "the jail they lived in was one they wanted to get out of; the one I kept talking about—the university—was one that I was working very hard to remain within."

Herron's Foucaultianism had enabled him "to feel as real to myself as I imagined the convicts to be: and whatever feeling I was looking for, I didn't find in the professional study of my subject, literature, at least not in the way I understood it. But as the subject of Foucault's disciplinary narcissism, I began to feel 'better' about myself, more significant, and in a position to meet the prisoners on their own ground." The passage gives a devastating picture of one motivation underlying the recent academic Foucault cult. Yet Herron does not reject the analysis of discursive power and ideology, but merely deploys it without foreordained conclusions.

Another way in which Herron's argument differs from that of the cultural right is in his recognition of the need for educators to build on the forms of literacy that already exist among students. Nothing could be more self-defeating than the right's dogmatic refusal to see the currently expanding study of popular culture and media as anything but a vulgar debasement of standards. For it is foolish to try to teach high culture without taking advantage of its relations to the culture with which students are already familiar. It is hardly a capitulation to vulgarity to recognize that education has to start with the interests and forms of consciousness already at hand. For Herron, such a principle means not replacing elite literacy with popular literacy, but making the two connected and concurrent parts of the common context of intellectual work. His most trenchant observation here is that in a society where high culture has traditionally been condescended to (recall the "Arts and Leisure" syndrome again), connecting high with popular culture is reasonably viewed not as a debasement but a step upward.

The split between high and mass culture is another expression of the disabling split between culture and work that is at the center of Herron's diagnosis. But for Herron the culture/work split is nowhere more vividly dramatized than in the English department hierarchy which assigns courses in literary subjects to the "regular" faculty and relegates the teaching of composition to graduate students and part-timers. Some of Herron's most biting pages deal with the situation of this new academic proletariat of itinerant composition-teachers, whom he likens to the aspiring actors who wait tables in a Broadway deli, who "don't really work here" and "are just hanging on, looking for their big break." In such comments, one feels that Herron speaks for the authentic experience of institutions like Wayne State University, an experience more representative of teaching conditions in the country at large than that of the Princetons, Harvards, and Yales. Herron recognizes that the widening gulf between academic haves and have-nots is partly a result of economic constraints, but he suggests that it is also a result of the university's failure to exploit the potential interconnectedness of different forms of intellectual work.

The split between composition and literature, like that between high and mass culture (or that between research and teaching), is unlikely to be healed (or made use of as a potentially instructive opposition) until universities come to terms with the problem of symbolic representation Herron describes. To put it another way, such splits will not be made to disappear by moral exhortation unaccompanied by structural changes in the collective organization of teaching. They are inevitable as long as there is no mediating intellectual culture—no common conversation or debate—to which the individual components of the university contribute.

Here I may be substituting my own analysis for Herron's, but it seems to me that the problem of making the humanities more responsive to the needs of society is usually thought about unproductively, and this is because of the tendency to confuse educational effectiveness with *teaching*. That is to say, we tend to reduce a problem of organizational structure to a problem of individual classroom behavior, assuming that the quality of education received by students is a function of the conduct of individual teachers rather than of the entire institution as it represents itself to outsiders. This superficial way of thinking causes us to blame the failure of the disciplines to communicate effectively to lay audiences on the notorious susceptibility of professors to technical jargon and esoteric or superspecialized methodologies. What this standard diagnosis cannot explain is how the philosophy and culture of the past ever managed to be transmitted, for it too, from Aristotle to Kant to Marx, has been technical, esoteric, and superspecialized. Is Derrida's *Of Grammatology* really that much more difficult than Aristotle's *Metaphysics*?

To account for the peculiar problems of transmission experienced by the modern academic disciplines, I would suggest that we need to direct our attention away from their intrinsic content (which is not self-evidently more esoteric than it has been in the past) to the diversification of these disciplines and the way the resulting diversity and conflict has been organized, or misorganized, in universities. What I am suggesting is that the diversification of the disciplines (and of the ideological and methodological premises of the disciplines) has reached a point where their organization into disparate and uncorrelated research "fields" has become counter-educational. To put it more simply, the connection and correlation of knowledge has not kept pace with its accumulation and expansion.

It is easy for an institution to transmit a difficult idea if every member is expounding (or at least relating themselves to) that same idea. To take a hypothetical situation, if all professors of literature were suddenly to become deconstructionists (I am not recommending this), students would quickly learn what deconstruction is. The nature of literary study itself would cease to be as mysterious as it has been even when "traditional" literary study was in the saddle, for it would manifest itself visibly through repetition and redundancy as one kind of thing—deconstruction. What makes literary study impenetrable to outsiders is not the advent of methodologies such as deconstruction, but the overlay of such methodologies on other very different ones with little help given to students in correlating the aggregate.

In other words, once literature professors have ceased being any single kind of thing, but come as deconstructionists, feminists, formalists, humanists, Marxists, historians, and many other types, the messages beamed out to students tend to get in one another's way rather than create redundancy and reinforcement. Unless corresponding efforts are made to increase the redundancy of the message, outsiders (or even insiders) will be unable to perceive what literary study is all about, for indeed that study has ceased to be "all about" any one thing that can be undisputably defined by a single party. Here is a schematic example of Herron's problem of symbolic representation.

The cultural right proposes a simple way to increase redundancy in the system: simply discourage (erase?) all the distracting, erroneous approaches to literature cluttering the landscape and reorganize literary studies around the correct, true approaches—those approaches (and those forms of literature) that meet the approval of the cultural right. Unfortunately, the spokesmen for the right fail to say what is to be done when the identity of the correct, true approaches to literature is vigorously contested within the faculty. Unless what is to be done is expel the dissenters, and that, as I noted earlier, is an imputation to which the right responds with indignation.

A more practical and democratic way to increase the redundancy of the system would be not to restrict the diversity of methodological and canonical options, but to see how better use might be made of that diversity. The result of such a tactic would be "pluralistic" insofar as it would take for granted that in a democratic culture there will be a plurality of literary traditions, views of literature, ideas of value, methods of approach, and ideological positions. The only alternative I can imagine to this sense of "pluralism" is dogmatism. But the point would be to go beyond the traditional form of academic pluralism by engaging the pluralities in a conversation. That is, the usual evasive and non-communicating pluralism would be replaced with a plurality of disagreements where conflicts are confronted and worked through in the open, and students and other outsiders would be able to see what is at stake in them and begin to take an interest in them.

What the outcome would be politically of such a reorganization in the collective relations of scholars is not necessarily predictable, but it would not have to be in order to be educationally effective. The point is to transform the university from the largely illegible text that it now is into a text that outsiders can read. In Herron's terms, this does not mean getting professors to do some one kind of thing as opposed to what they now do. It means making the whole of the university and the humanities more coherently representative of the culture of intellectual work they actually contain. Only then will we be in a position to see what our humanistic culture may be good for.

Gerald Graff

Acknowledgments

I wish to thank my colleagues Charlie Baxter, Gerald MacLean, Arthur Marotti, and Ross Pudaloff for their suggestions, advice, and general support. I am also grateful to Jerry Graff and Mark Shechner, who read my manuscript and made valuable suggestions. Robert Mandel and Lee Schreiner, at the Wayne State University Press, have been good friends to me and my work. I owe them a debt of thanks. For their editorial assistance, I am grateful to Laurel Brandt and Robert S. Demorest.

To an old, good friend, Mary Burgan, thanks and thanks again.

Harold Schechter has been a colleague, a generous critic and supporter, and a friend. His kindness to me has been unstinting. I shall always be grateful for the many things he has done.

I am grateful too to Wayne State University for financial support and time off.

Introduction

Though it may not be impossible to imagine what the word *culture* means, it is surely difficult to imagine the thing itself existing within, or because of, the university, especially a contemporary American one. Never mind the students, whom the institution is so stupendously supposed to have failed, as per the testimony of the College Board, the secretary of education, the Carnegie Commission, the Rockefeller Foundation, and a host of others. The familiar scandal of pedagogical profligacy is pretty well summed up by Allan Bloom, whose book *The Closing of the American Mind*[1] spent half of 1987 on the *New York Times* list of best-sellers. He explains, according to his subtitle, "how higher education has failed democracy and impoverished the souls of today's students." Never mind those students, though, at least for the moment. If the university stands for culture, as a lot of people have imagined it to do—perhaps since the Middle Ages but surely since the time of Matthew Arnold—then where among its inmates is culture to be found?

For the people who work in a university, this is an amusing question. Is it *you* who is the repository of culture? Or is it your friend in economics? or your antagonist in biology? Maybe it's the dean of liberal arts who stands for culture. Or maybe the president of the university? Is the football coach part of culture, and are the engineers? If they aren't, then why are they kept around, given what the college catalog says about liberal education, intellectual horizons, and so on? These questions, of course, are absurd. It's not any one

23

in particular, but all of them/us together. Taken together, the assembled faculties of the university represent in large the faculties of a cultivated, a cultured, individual. We stand for a potential, an ideal, that perhaps no one individually will ever achieve.

Well, maybe—although, if taken seriously, this representational model turns out even more absurd than the personal version of culture. Take E. D. Hirsch's book, for example (also a best-seller), *Cultural Literacy: What Every American Needs to Know*.[2] There's a discursive argument about what people ought to know and why, if they are to be considered cultured. But the real fun is Hirsch's appendix, "The List," which is a sixty-four-page (double column) enumeration of dates, names, and phrases. According to the author and his collaborators, they "do not seek to create a complete catalogue of American knowledge but to establish guideposts that can be of practical use to teachers, students, and all others who need to know our literate culture" (p. 146). Disclaimers aside, though, is that what culture means? Being able to identify "pagoda (image)" and "Paine, Thomas"? The assumption, at any rate—an assumption fundamental to the representational model of a university—is that it is. The various faculties keep alive, and pass along, the references that, taken together, stand for culture. As a friend of mine said, Hirsch's project makes an interesting board game, but the game would be more fun if it included sports and entertainment. By which I suppose he means that the football coach ought to be a part of culture too.

Obviously, there's more to "culture" than simple mnemonic skill, as even Hirsch admits. But what precisely does that something else consist of? One might answer as Matthew Arnold did by referring to the "best self," which is all to the good, except when it comes to defining the best self, which only moves things back to square one. T. S. Eliot, who can usually be relied upon in these matters, said the following in his "Notes towards the Definition of Culture":

> The reflection that what we believe is not merely what we formulate and subscribe to, but that behaviour is also belief, and that even the most conscious and developed of us live also at the level on which belief and behaviour cannot be distinguished, is one that may, once we allow our imagination to play upon it, be very disconcerting. It gives an importance to our most trivial pursuits, to the occupation of our every minute, which we cannot contemplate long without the horror of nightmare.[3]

Indeed. Which is why I find Hirsch's pursuits—or rather their obvious popularity—both trivial and also upsetting. If behavior is a form of belief, as Eliot supposed, could one, or should one, possibly believe in the value of an institution set up to model a Yuppie board game? As the drive toward some sort of standardized, national testing of education gathers strength, the answer disturbingly seems to be *yes*. And it is our own secretary of education, William Bennett, who is championing this cause. But supposing we just say *no* to the Bennett/Hirsch option, what then? Well, there is always poetry, which was Arnold's answer to the puzzle of culture, or the Church of England, which was Eliot's. Neither, however, seems to have much to do with contemporary American universities or the lives of the citizens they ostensibly serve. So where is culture?

Perhaps it would be better to ask *what* it is. That question is much easier to answer. Culture is what professors claim to believe in when things go wrong, and wrong is how things generally go around the academy. In that, all the experts agree—if not by precept, certainly by example. Like health, culture is something you don't think too much about unless you haven't got it. But my comparison is not quite accurate because the people who worry about culture usually worry not about themselves but about other people's state of being. And for practical purposes, that state is almost always described in terms of decline. Culture, then, is the finest form of presumptive nostalgia: the longing we imagine others would feel if they only realized the value of things they never knew about, but now seem disastrously to have "forgotten." It's amusing in that connection to contemplate the number of culture's heroes and heroines who would have turned up illiterates if they'd been forced to pass Hirsch's quiz, or its contemporary equivalent. No matter. They don't need us; it's we who need them, particularly once they have lapsed from popularity into academic repose, because without their posthumous service, there could be no culture. At any rate, there could be no university. The academy—or I should say, the culture-generating part of the academy—is based not on belief, which is where Eliot and Arnold among others have mistaken us; the academy is a managerial institution in which belief is irrelevant, if not an outright hindrance.

We trade in materials that have outlived their usefulness, if in fact they ever had any. For academic purposes, popular subjects, much less a whole "popular culture," would never do. After all, the power of trivial pursuits, whether institutional or recreational, depends on a public demonstration of ignorance rather than knowledge. This is why crisis, instead of competence, dictates the organizing agenda of academies. The point is a simple one, but it is very little understood.

Whatever the calamities that a deprivation of culture is supposed to induce—and they are legion, as per the prognosis of Hirsch,
Bloom, and company—the present is apparently neither better nor
worse off than the past. Not, at any rate, with regard to the cultivation
of such humane virtues as generosity, pity, love, or kindness. And
the great evil democratizer—global nuclear destruction—was
brought to us by people all of whom had the benefit of advanced
academic culture: people who went to school back before grade
inflation, when things were good. So what then? Not surprisingly,
the university is not startled by the apparent contradictions of its
position. It, like the Tar Baby, is not to be confounded.

As a matter of fact, universities couldn't get along without an
ever renewable supply of crises, because crisis is the only sure way
of keeping culture alive, which is the point of Hirsch's "List," and
the anxiety that it and similar lists have induced in the minds of
governors, congressmen, parents, and the secretary of education. If
ours is a culture that no single person contains, and that institutional
aggregates cannot empirically demonstrate, what means can there be
for proving its existence, or for justifying the money spent in its
support? There would be none, except for the crisis narratives that
induce from particular, negative evidence a reality that might otherwise remain unknowable. Any failure of consensus is transformed
into an inverse proof of culture: SAT scores decline because of a
lapse of culture; people don't read as much as they used to because
they have no culture; kids in school can't pass trivial pursuit *id*
quizzes because the culture has dissolved. The more pronounced the
absence of culture, the more powerful its presumption becomes. By
this logic, the worse things get, the greater the need for, and the
consequent value of, culture, so that it behooves academics to spread
as much bad news as they can invent. In the process the locus of
culture necessarily and conveniently recedes into the past, where it
can't be examined firsthand. We invoke the memory of how good
things used to be in order to show how bad they are now, and more
importantly to valorize a particular vision of the future, a vision
vouchsafed only to "us." This is why the proponents of crisis tend
to be both powerful and conservative: members of the academic
"establishment," in other words. They have the most to lose if
conditions change; and they recognize crisis for what it is, which is
a potent instrument of control, both inside the academy and outside
it.

There is a problem with arguments for a golden age, however:
they presume past glories to have been the effect of institutional

causes. But this connection is never demonstrated, nor can it be. For one thing, the institutions presumed to have functioned with such internal coherence and normative sway probably never existed in the first place.[4] And even if they had, they never involved more than a small minority of the population concentrated mostly on the East Coast. For good or ill, then, the past cannot be ascribed to the influence of institutions that the majority of people had no experience of. Interestingly, it is the point when universities actually became an ideological, if not actual, part of middle-class experience, some time after World War II, that most crisis narratives identify as the beginning of the end of the good old days. As with most myths, the less one knows or cares about the facts, the better the story becomes.

By which I don't mean to imply that I don't believe there is such a thing as culture, because I do, after a fashion. At least, I believe the university ought to take seriously the cultural agenda it has espoused for the last hundred years. Nor do I mean to imply that I don't believe the university is in crisis, because it is. Ours is not just any old crisis, however. Rather than evincing a failure of expertise, our predicament is the direct result of it. There are right now, for instance, more literacy specialists per capita in the United States than at any time in the history of human societies, just as the number of living humanities majors and professors exceeds the historical total of people who have ever taught or studied that field. Rather than solving problems, however, all we specialists are presiding over a mess: a crisis both public and professional, as even the most casual newspaper reader is probably aware. Which might lead a person to wonder why the widest dispersal of professorial culture in human history has yielded not a literate society but an illiterate one, presided over institutionally by professionals apparently incapable of teaching what they profess. Thus far I would agree at least with the implication of popular mythology. My disagreement comes with regard to intention. The crisis we confront is not the result of academic lapse; on the contrary, it represents the outward triumph of professorial culture—a triumph that might end up costing a lot of us our jobs.

In his study *Professing Literature*, Gerald Graff investigates the reasons why the institutionalization of culture, specifically literary culture, has rendered it trivial, and consequently prone to mythological intervention. As Graff sees it, our problems originate with the field-coverage model of academic organization: the notion that literature—or culture in general, for that matter—should be organized institutionally by first dividing it into separate fields, and then assigning individual instructors to "cover" each of these fields. The result is highly efficient managerially, but intellectually bland because the animating differences and controversies that inform cultural life are rendered invisible, except to professionals, which is why it has become so difficult to imagine what, *in the world,* culture might be good for:

> The field-coverage principle made the modern educational machine friction free, for by making individuals functionally independent in the carrying out of their tasks it prevented conflicts from erupting which would otherwise have had to be confronted, debated, and worked through. An invisible hand . . . saw to it that the sum of the parts added up to a coherent whole. . . . To put it another way, the field-coverage principle enabled administrative organization to take the place of principled thought and discussion.[5]

The same might be said of academic culture in general. As Graff suggests, "culture," like "literature"—if properly understood—is not so much a problem as it is a problematic—a way of posing questions, potentially important questions, about language, history, work, memory, class, and so on. But given the present constitution of academies, such questions are not likely to come up.

For example, the discursive prominence of culture itself raises the question whether all of "us" ought to belong to a single thing. This is a question of special relevance in America, where the ideology, if not the fact, of democracy has achieved its greatest modern currency. Ought we be representable in institutional terms? Institutionally, at least, the answer is *yes*, if one trusts the discourse by which institutions account for themselves. The proponents of crisis urge the same point with a hysterical intensity. However, even the most casual, practical examination of institutions exposes the lies on which crisis depends, and the bad faith that conscious lying breeds. Contrary to popular mythology, there is a significant degree of fiscal good health (thanks largely to the arrival of baby boom progeny), but there is an utter failure to achieve, or even to desire, in real terms the philosophical coherence that catalogs proclaim. And this is probably a good thing. What is not good is the way that the incoherence of institutions is "covered." Our situation is the result not of disinterest so much as disconnection, which is Gerald Graff's point.

By default, then, the academic bureaucracy—comprised of department chairs, deans, provosts, presidents—is allowed and/or compelled to answer for, to represent, in terms of bland coherence, the professionals who nominally contain culture, the majority of whom would disagree—even violently—about the proper meaning of a national life, and about the texts that ought to be its basis. Crisis, by virtue of its convenient *absence* of culture, provides a timely alternative, should actual disputes occur. It's the one thing everybody *can* agree on because it represents nothing more than a heuristic, empty category. But crisis or no, people both inside and outside the academy might reasonably assume that confrontations never happen except in oddball places like Yale, or France; and in language that no common person and few professionals (except for specialists in the "field") can understand. There are fights, sure—about money, power, enrollment, teaching loads, parking space—but never any public, local disputations about culture, or about the content of one's "real work." Which leads to the utterly ridiculous conclusion that "we" are basically in agreement. And that is an obvious and dangerous lie.

But it is one that we allow to go on, that we even support by not intervening in each other's lives. Only the "great" figures rise from their field-coverage niches to regale each other at national meetings, or in the pages of the *New York Review of Books,* wherein academic differences of opinion achieve in the minds of the majority of citizens the status of comic opera. Or what would be more accurate to say, wherein the stuff of academic representations yields—at least potentially—to a cartoonizing superficiality, since most people neither know nor care about professorial debates or the individuals who engage in them. It's no accident, then, that the *New York Review,* with all its intellectual pretensions, has also made the career of the brilliant cartoonist David Levine. But this cartoonizing of culture is nothing to be proud of, or even indifferent to. However ridiculous the atmospherics, and language, of professorial debates may appear, they engage topics of vital concern to a society such as ours, particularly to members of the middle class, the representable security of whose culture is very much in question.

The confirmation hearings of Judge Robert Bork offer a rare instance of academic translation, when scholarly questions got looked at as if they matter in the real world, which obviously they do, to great numbers of people. The debates that arose over the hearings demonstrate clearly enough the problematic nature of culture, or a national life, and of the institutions that claim to represent it coherently. But Bork's hearings present a rare case. By contrast, the atmosphere in which academic debates are usually conducted renders them irrelevant generally in two important ways. First, as I've suggested, few people can comprehend them, thanks to the prestige jargons of field specialization—jargons encouraged by the economy of academic publication. Second, because of the mutual assured banality of the field-coverage model, such debates rarely occur at home, where just anybody might listen in; nor do they include experience that is merely "popular," which is to say the recognizable content of everyday life. As a result, the potential relevance of our cultural problematic is reduced to superfluity and special pleading.

Even when the agents of culture interest themselves in real life, as Allan Bloom does, the rhetoric of crisis typically proves more powerful than critical intelligence. There is, for example, Bloom's indictment of rock and roll, the consumers of which he portrays as the ungrateful inheritors of the economic plenty and technological progress represented by American "culture." "And in what does progress culminate," Bloom asks:

> A pubescent child whose body throbs with orgasmic rhythms; whose feelings are made articulate in hymns to the joys of onanism or the killing of parents; whose ambition is to win fame and wealth in imitating the drag-queen who makes the music. In short, life is made into a nonstop, commercially prepackaged masturbational fantasy. (P. 75)

Such gross generalizations—which go entirely unsupported—are not likely to win much popular respect for academic intelligence, or for the people who represent it. For instance, Jon Pareles, writing for the *New York Times,* has pointed out that the average consumer of rock is not a child but an adult in her/his twenties, thirties, or forties (p. 30). (Secretary Bennett, for instance, is an avowed fan of Bloom's "commercially prepackaged masturbational" fantasies.) Furthermore, Pareles objects, reasonably, to Bloom's lack of evidence. "Perhaps [Bloom] can explain how Bob Dylan's 'Like a Rolling Stone,' Led Zeppelin's 'Stairway to Heaven,' Grandmaster Flash's 'Message' and Suzanne Vega's 'Luka,' to name only a few random hits, are all onanistic fantasies."[6] The point, of course, is that he can't; and as far as the culture he is hysterically defending is concerned, it doesn't matter. Bloom doesn't want or need to know anything about the differences that animate contemporary life, which defines a society, perhaps, but certainly not a "culture." Consequently, he can get away with a cheap reductionism that would cause him no end of grief if it were ever to occur in his real work, which is philosophy. Of course, if Bloom took philosophy no more seriously than he does contemporary America, he'd never get published in the first place.

All of which merely goes to support the myth of cultural superfluity, which is the popular obverse of the myth of cultural decline. The professors despair of, and mythologize, the decline of culture. But thanks to professional disdain, people who are apparently forever to be excluded from its nostalgic pleasures tend to think such exclusion doesn't matter. The organization of institutions and the pop-cultural slumming of somebody like Bloom only act to support such myths. As a result, the questions posed by culture never get asked in ways that will make a difference.

If things are to change, academics will have to behave differently, particularly with regard to culture. To begin with, it would be advisable to think of culture not as a text, or texts, but as a stage for confronting the contradictions that the ideal, or ideology, is meant to conceal. Culture can, perhaps, be staged, but it can no longer be transmitted textually because such transmission presumes a consensus and a common literacy. Whether these existed in the past is dubious. That they don't now is clear. Even the staunchest true believers are willing to concede as much. In that connection Arnold perhaps understood more than he is sometimes credited with, or more than he himself was aware of. He titled his pamphlet "Culture and Anarchy," and that linkage deserves consideration. Anarchy is a matter far different from the chimerical figure of "crisis," which offers no real opposition at all but merely a cover-up for ignorance and pretension. By contrast, Arnold's opposition suggests a potential truth that is available only in active presentation, or confrontation; just as he never would have discovered culture in the first place if it hadn't been for a group of anarchic protesters who tore down the railings in Hyde Park. As this paradigmatic event suggests, there is nothing positive to tell about culture. Instead, it—like Hyde Park—is merely a *space* where people can act.

If universities exist in the present, then so must the culture they/we purvey, along with the subjects on whose behalf we supposedly act and remember. The past may be prologue, as Shakespeare says, but too often nobody bothers with the rest of the story. If culture involves knowing things, we ought to begin by asking what we know, all of us collectively if not together, rather than inventing more ways of measuring what other people don't know about the past, and probably never did know. Then maybe we can get around to figuring out what, if anything, the institutionalized past is good for. Otherwise, the possibility of engagement with everyday life is lost, the chance of genuine entitlement is denied. But these losses become unhappy only if read in the context of hope, which it has been the project of culture, more often than not, to dismantle.

In the essay that follows I examine the "crisis" we are in and the history that got us into it. And I look at the effects our situation has on the academic profession, and particularly on the relations between teachers and students. My argument is that the university no longer works; it no longer represents the culture that it nominally serves and is supported by. In a middle-class society based on information and service, the work of Matthew Arnold's production-based culture has been done. It is a superfluous venture, therefore, to preserve this outmoded subject. And not only that: a bankrupt culture now occupies and falsifies the stage on which we might otherwise act out the confrontation of institutional memory with actual social practice. As a result of this representational failure on the part of the university, people are left stranded, without anything to belong to except a mythic past about which they know very little other than what the media tells them. It is my belief that something ought to be done; it's my hope that something will be done—and not by the people who usually end up doing all the practical (and ultimately decisive) jobs that academics say they don't have time for. Either way, what we've got doesn't work, and it ought to be changed because none of us deserves so expensive a mess, despite our having earned it.

1. Crisis

Cardinal Newman was right—prophetic might be a better word. He wanted a liberal education based on "knowledge as its own end"; that was his central, his "universal" idea. And that's just what we've got, for good or ill. "Things which can bear to be cut off from everything else and yet persist in living must have life in themselves," he wrote: "Pursuits, which issue in nothing, and still maintain their ground for ages, which are regarded as admirable, though they have not yet proved themselves to be useful, must have their sufficient end in themselves, whatever it turn out to be."[1] His version of liberal education has become *the* version—at least based on the empirical data available—so that people involved with the liberal arts find themselves in a position to judge the "sufficient end" of knowledge, now that there has been time to find what that end turns out to be. Here's one characteristically unstartling conclusion from the Rockefeller Commission on the Humanities, who were among the first contributors to a now extensive anthology of contemporary lamentation: "Free to choose, students [in the past decade] chose vocationalism. Liberal education and the humanities, their fates still linked, were willed to the periphery of undergraduate learning."[2] Cardinal Newman wanted liberal education to be special, to be set apart. Now it surely is that.

The question is what "we" are going to do about it—we who work at the university. As regards the place of literary study specifically, producers have beèn as quick—if not so enthusiastic—as consumers at detecting, and elaborating, the "admirable" isolation of their endeavors, "which issue in nothing and still maintain their ground for ages." Helene Moglen, writing for *Profession 83,* summed the case up pretty well in a journal whose pages, more often than not, are devoted to questioning whether the "profession" it nominally represents still meaningfully exists: "Education is in trouble, and the humanities are in the greatest trouble of all. . . . Students, parents, and university administrators have lost faith in the value of our forms of knowledge. More seriously, humanists have lost faith in themselves as they have watched their values and modes of inquiry lose influence while they themselves have become marginalized in the schools and in society at large."[3] Post-modernist America has not proved a hospitable place, or "space," for humanists, though even these times are not without certain giddy, if ephemeral, exhilarations. In his recent book, *The Post-Modern Aura,* Charles Newman has noted the tendency, among post-humanists, toward "the development of secondary languages which presumably 'demystify' reality, but actually tend to further obscure it. In such a situation, both the critical and the aesthetic intelligence often relinquish their traditional claims, preferring to explore what they imagine to be the richness of their own limitations."[4] Yet even now, in these days of post-traditional apostasy and intentional limitation, the humanities "persist in living."

In fact, there even appears to be a nascent renewal under way, if the ascendancy of William J. Bennett—once head of the National Endowment, and lately secretary of education—is in any sense indicative. Surely there must be hope for everyone who draws pay for teaching the liberal arts. And that is good news. But hope of what sort? That's another question entirely.

Lionel Trilling was a man well acquainted with liberal education, and with the price one often has to pay in order to espouse its cause; he said this in his essay, "The Meaning of a Literary Idea": "To call ourselves the people of the idea is to flatter ourselves. We are rather the people of ideology, which is a very different thing. Ideology is not the product of thought; it is the habit or the ritual of showing respect for certain formulas to which, for various reasons having to do with emotional safety, we have very strong ties, of whose meaning and consequences in actuality we have no clear understanding."[5] For various reasons having to do with emotional safety, it has been comfortable for academics, historically, to think of themselves as being cut off: a kind of wilderness-loving, prophetic elite.

Following this classic, Newman line, it is precisely the being "cut off from everything else" that endows the liberal arts with their special status and power: like gold they retain value because they are distinct from the shifting currency of everyday knowledge. Their moment of production is distant in time, and not subject to present manipulation (any more than the earth's supply of precious metals, which can neither be added to nor detracted from, though they can, of course, be reapportioned). The "truth" of humane knowledge therefore offers a hedge against what Charles Newman refers to as the inflationary pressures of post-modernism. Provided, of course, that the liberal arts, like the gold standard, "persist in living," which is to say, provided that they retain their privilege, ideologically, as the natural resort of a desire for fixed standards. But desire is apparently the problem, the source of that self-conscious "crisis" that now attracts so much attention. Humanists may be members of a prophetic elite, but their truths won't do anybody much good, themselves included, if people in general forget how to need the security that the liberal arts, and those who serve them, are capable of providing.

Something ought to be done, so the classic line goes, and professors—supposedly—are just the people to do it. I quote once more from the report of the Commission on the Humanities:

> The humanities have always been associated with the civic purpose of liberal education—to prepare the individual for making informed choices and acting responsibly. This purpose must be reasserted today, with special urgency. As instant communications deluge us with information on social and political issues, we face civic choices more complex and perhaps more numerous than ever before. The humanities emphasize interpretation and criticism, indispensable techniques for participating in community life and keeping watch over its values. (Pp. 69–70)

An informational deluge threatens to overwhelm us with unprecedented complexities, and there's much work to be done—work that requires a sense of fixed, critical values with which to oppose the dangerous, inflationary flux.

This "diagnosis" ought by now to be familiar to anybody who reads the newspapers, not to mention professional and scholarly journals, where it is rehearsed weekly by various panels, commissions, and public officials.[6] We are, as the much quoted National Commission on Excellence in Education has put it, "a nation at risk." For the first time in a long time, education is front page news, which is where the commission's findings got reported in the *New York Times:* "If an unfriendly foreign power had attempted to impose on America the mediocre educational performance that exists today, we might well have viewed it as an act of war. As it stands, we have allowed this to happen to ourselves."[7] That day (27 April 1983), there also appeared, on the same page, stories about aid to the embattled Salvadoran government and a hunt being conducted by the Swedish navy to locate some Soviet minisubs that they suspected of spying. Our enemies are all around us, and there was the evidence to prove it. The "Evil Empire," as President Reagan refers to it, has apparently got more, or at least more concerted, friends than we do. And what is perhaps worst of all, their nefarious aims are being abetted by our own lackadaisical attitude. According to the Carnegie Forum's report, "A Nation Prepared": "The nationwide effort to improve our schools and student achievement rivals those of any period in American history. . . . But more will be required, much more than could have been imagined just a few years ago."[8] If we're going to survive, then we'll have to get it together, as the saying goes; and that turns out to be very good news indeed for the liberal arts, along with those who practice them.

Given their "traditional" commitment to those "indispensable techniques for participating in community life and keeping watch over its values," it's only natural that humanists ought to respond to the crisis that threatens us all. Thus far, though, that response has generally consisted of reproducing, in terms specially relevant to their own survival, the same narrative agenda by means of which the need for commitments is to be discovered in the first place. As with any other kind of product, from high-fiber cereal to stealth bombers, the value of a liberal education cannot be realized until potential clients are made aware of their own state of deprivation and the dire consequences that may attend upon a failure to consume. Present conditions merely make it possible to urge this public-spirited message in a specially forceful way. The professors are not being called back by the culture at large, in other words—at least not yet. The crisis in (and on behalf of) academe is still largely one of their own contriving, as the membership rosters of the various commissions and panels will show.

So, they—we—persist. Our proleptic ventriloquizing—our letting the world discover, in newspapers and magazines and on television, how much we can imagine its discovering it needs us—has developed rich mythological and literary trappings so that the voice of nature appears spontaneously, and anxiously, to recite our own job descriptions. It is the "nation" that is said to be at risk, for example, rather than the jobs of certain professors who live in it. But for the most part, the "crisis" in the humanities—or rather the energy required to produce that crisis—is just so much wasted effort. As far as practical realities are concerned, our so-called crisis is a bunch of bunk, an "ideological" chimera, as Trilling might say, though, like other bad dreams, it is perhaps no less a source of enlightenment for all that.

By this I don't mean that there aren't ever crises in education. The United States had a real crisis in the 1960s, and early 1970s, when nobody even knew one was occurring, or else didn't care: probably because the crisis at that point felt a great deal more like success, a success produced by the collegiate arrival of the postwar baby boom. This group, which is and will remain the largest demographic cohort throughout the lifetime of any American presently living, began reaching college in the first half of the 1960s, creating the greatest enrollment increase in history, so that by 1969 higher education employed more workers than either the automotive or steel industries.[9] There truly was a crisis at that point, but it was one of undersupply, not oversupply. Colleges had to cope with an unprecedented demand for their facilities and services, which is precisely what they did, with the result that by 1975, one-quarter of all people ages 25–29 had completed at least four years of higher education (Jones, p. 180). At about that point, graduates began encountering the inevitable problems of oversupply, particularly holders of advanced degrees in the humanities, for whom academic work was essentially the only source of employment. They were the product of institutions that had geared up in order to accommodate an unprecedented growth in enrollments. Once the numbers of entering students began to level off, and then to decline, as the demographic bulge made its way through the collegiate boa constrictor, there was no longer a special need for new Ph.D.'s. In fact, colleges would encounter increasing difficulty just finding students for the faculty they already had in place and tenured.

The net result of this change has been a better educated, though increasingly underemployed, population. According to one estimate, between 1976 and 1985, 10.4 million college graduates competed for 7.7 million jobs traditionally filled by people with degrees, which means that 2.7 million degree-holders failed to find employment commensurate with their academic preparation (Jones, p. 181). Humanities graduates have been less fortunate than most, with holders of Ph.D.'s doing the worst of all, since they are prepared to do only one thing. Representative of this problem are such academic repackaging manuals as one very good one written by Dorothy K. Bestor, *Aside*

from Teaching, What in the World Can You Do? That has become
the question for a great many people these days. In her book Bestor
offers both consolation and some practical advice. She also cites
studies of the contemporary academic marketplace to the effect that
between 1980 and 2000, only one in ten holders of humanities doc-
torates will ever find academic employment, with not all of these
finding jobs leading to tenure and a permanent career.[10] What this all
comes down to is a gross deprofessionalization of liberal arts degrees
in general, and Ph.D.'s in particular. The figures may vary slightly
one way or the other, but it's a fact either way that the majority of
people holding professional credentials in the liberal arts will never
practice their nominal profession.

    Given this context, our contemporary "crisis" seems more to
parody the facts than represent them, though not without reason.
Panel after panel of academics lament the waning of the liberal arts
at the precise moment when more Americans have experience of
them than at any point in human history. There has never been, nor
will there be, a people so conversant, statistically, with the liberal
arts. Obviously, then, our crisis is not precisely what it purports to
be. Naturally, the people who want academic work but fail to find it
are having a genuine crisis of significant personal dimensions. I do
not mean to diminish their predicament, or the responsibility of those
who might have known better and resisted the temptation of short-
term growth and quick-yield profits that the pre-recession 1960s and
1970s offered. But "humanists" are no better than anybody else, as
everyone has known all along, though we generally prefer to think,
and say, otherwise, which is the basis of our current claim that the
American people need more of what they already have an unprecedented surplus of. And in any case, the vast majority of college
graduates—even in the liberal arts—are still finding jobs of some
sort; and with the present recovery under way, even more of them
will be doing so.

    Despite the usual claims, therefore, our crisis has less to do
with life "out there" in the world, either substantively or vocationally, than it does with academic professionals' relation to that life.
The authority, and the value, of academe can be maintained only so
long as we have something that other people want and are willing to
pay for because they need it. What has happened now is that more
than half of the Ph.D. holders in American history are currently
living, and most of them work not inside the university but outside
it. There has perhaps never been a greater dispersal of humane letters
since Henry VIII dissolved the monasteries, which produced the

same problem—the *real* problem—confronting people who continue to staff the institutions of church and state.[11] Given the ubiquity of the liberal arts, and professional degree–holders, what is the work of institutional academics now to represent, and how ought we represent it to the people whose own work must pay our bills, many of them holders of the same credentials we have? The response to this question can be summarized in one word that is also the title of a journal published annually by the Modern Language Association, the appearance of which in 1977 dates the inception of our contemporary agenda of crisis: *Profession.*

If our aim is the dissemination of "culture," to use Arnold's term, then the humanities have never been more secure. If, on the other hand, our aim is the preservation of a professional academism, then we—the professional academics—are in trouble. More than any other profession, ours has come to represent the surrender to inflationary pressures against which traditional values are meant to be a stay. Doctors, even lawyers, don't have the kind of problems we do because they have been better at self-regulation, which led Neal Woodruff to the following conclusion in the inaugural issue of *Profession:* "I believe we should begin work immediately toward a national advisory quota system for admissions to graduate study in the modern languages."[12] No such system was ever undertaken, nor is it likely to be. Instead, we have chosen to manage ourselves by means of a crisis that sustains (quite opportunely) the same inflationary conditions that we nominally claim to deplore.

As I've suggested, a Ph.D. in the humanities is, strictly speaking, no longer a professional degree because the great majority of people holding one (or of those who will hold one in the future) are not professionals, nor will they ever be.[13] There is little likelihood that study (on whatever level) in this already overstudied field will bear any relation to one's future work. But at least since World War II, it has been work, or the desire for *good* work, that brought people to college in the first place, so that knowledge which is no longer working is in danger of extinction.

The present economic transformation, coupled with the proportionate shrinking of federal funding for education, will not likely increase the public's taste for superfluity, particularly when so many of them have had the benefit of seeing up close what it is that we do. There's no reason why academic production should be protected when other production is not. Therefore, in order to sustain a professional class based on the overproduction of an already devalued commodity—whether conceived as the things we know, or the train-

ing required to know them—some system of difference is required
to make what is already out there different from what is about to be.
That is where crisis comes in. The thing that makes academic insiders
different from outsiders, and therefore deserving of support, is that
"we" understand crisis and, by definition, "they" do not, because
if they did, they'd be in here with us. They become subject to our
narrative because "they" aren't here, where the writing gets done,
and "we" are. And as times get worse, which they are bound to do,
the more "they" are going to need our help, which is the brilliant
strategy discovered by our profession and our *Profession*; and that
is why both seem so preoccupied with bad news.

As it turns out, there is no neglected duty, no lost, or almost
lost, cause to be rallied around. We've been doing our job all along,
and we've been doing it very well. That's why America still has an
academy, despite our self-advertised superfluity; that's why people
with advanced degrees in fields such as literature continue to get jobs
and tenure. That's why any university that wants to be taken seriously nowadays must institute stronger, rather than weaker, humanities requirements, insisting on their relevance "across the curriculum." And finally, that's how the supposedly superfluous humanities
got Mr. Bennett his seat on the president's cabinet, from which
vantage he spins back, for our delectation, his tale of dangerous
abandonment. Business is good, in other words; but like our chief,
we cling to our "idea," our ideology, that is, of elegant, uncompro-
mised isolation: desperate living, with fringe benefits and a retirement
plan. So long as we continue in this illusory, if comforting, pose,
we'll be in no position to understand the nature of our work, and who
we work for—however consciously—and why, mysteriously, we
keep getting hired. I suspect we don't want to know too much about
those things, for reasons of "emotional safety," as Trilling said.

Like his intellectual patron Matthew Arnold, Trilling tried to
see the academic situation both steadily and whole, which occasioned
him no amount of grief (and awkward self-justification) in the 1950s
and again in the 1960s—and from the precise "ideological" cause
that Arnold warned against. For Arnold the object of professional
activity is "criticism," the chief virtue of which is "disinterestedness." "And how is criticism to show disinterestedness?" he asked:
"By keeping aloof from what is called 'the practical view of things';
by resolutely following the law of its own nature, which is to be a
free play of the mind on all subjects which it touches. . . . Its business
is . . . to leave alone all questions of practical consequences and
applications, questions which will never fail to have due prominence

given them.''[14] This is very close to Newman's idea of knowledge as its own end. Arnold suggests that we—as critics—do the talking, create the essential conditions of self-consciousness (''being something'') on which the life of ''culture'' depends, while others (intent upon ''having something'') are left to labor humbly over ''practical consequences and applications.'' We don't work, and they do. And that, more or less, is precisely what happens, or at least how it gets explained.

Here, for example, is Secretary Bennett on the same topic: ''Expanding on a phrase from Matthew Arnold, I would describe the humanities as the best that has been said, thought, written, and otherwise expressed about the human experience.''[15] So far, so good; but Bennett doesn't let the professionals off as easily as Arnold, who remains uninterested in the critic except as a writer or public figure. For reasons that I'll get to shortly, Bennett comes down as hard on those inside the academy as he does on the ignorant ''populace,'' who remain uncaringly, and dangerously, outside its cure. As to the efforts of those who convey the good news, ''disinterestedness'' is again essential, though not merely as an attribute of the Arnoldian discourse, criticism, but as the fundamental basis of pedagogical practice.

Teaching, in other words, must not emerge visibly, ideologically, as a motivated form of work (a working *for* one thing, or *against* another). That it has is one source of the crisis that now overtakes us, as Bennett and his ''Study Group on the State of Learning in the Humanities in Higher Education'' concluded: ''The study group was alarmed by the tendency of some humanities professors to present their subjects in a tendentious, ideological manner'' (p. 19). This is not to say that the humanities ought to be taught in a lifeless way; far from it: ''At the other extreme [from the ideological], the humanities are declared to have no inherent meaning because all meaning is subjective and relative to one's own perspective'' (p. 19). Enervation is no better than a misguidedly passionate intensity.

To be sure, the humanist/instructor must believe deeply in what he or she is doing, though this depth of commitment is to be expressed not discursively, but more as a certain, performative intensity: ''This does not mean that they [the teachers] advocate each idea of every author, but rather that they are moved and are seen to be moved by the power of the works and are able to convey that power to their students. Just as good scholarship is inspired, so must good teaching be'' (p. 17). Ideologically speaking, this position is not without its consolations, and supporters. The truths of our humanistic legacy are no more to be thought of as objects of production, of "artful" manufacture, than the value of gold is to be confused with the labor required to extract it from the earth. It is better to think of the "best," like the Kruggerand, as if it were self-generating: a "natural" stay against inflationary crisis. "Things, which can bear to be cut off from everything else and yet persist in living, must have life in themselves," as Cardinal Newman put it. Or if they don't, they ought to. Crisis, then, figures the ultimate redemption of academic endeavors; it elevates the practitioner—urgently, serviceably—above the terrain of mere ideology and self-seeking.

Summarizing, though not sympathizing with, this argument for the ideological innocence of academic work, Edward Said wrote that "the particular mission of the humanities is, in the aggregate, to represent *noninterference* in the affairs of the everyday world."[16] He made that charge in an essay published five years ago, the point of which was to oppose a depoliticizing of knowledge that he then saw under way: "What I argue, is that a particular situation within the field we call "criticism" is not merely related to but is an integral part of the currents of thought and practice that play a role within the Reagan era. Moreover, I think, "criticism" and the traditional academic humanities have gone through a series of developments over time whose beneficiary and culmination is Reaganism" (p. 1). At this point we have had some additional years and a second election against which to measure Said's conclusions, and though I agree with the connections he sets out to establish, I think he has failed to credit adequately the larger forces involved here. Ronald Reagan is not so much a culmination as he is a means toward an end, that end being the redefinition of work in a postindustrial, and permanently inflationary, atmosphere. And as of his reelection, and the elevation of Secretary Bennett, that task has largely been accomplished, at least so far as the humanities are concerned, so that the present "crisis" is not so much a warning of something about to happen as it is an indicator of something—something insistently unideological—that already has.

2. Work

Ours is a society grown accustomed—quite profitably—to extreme conditions. Far from terrorizing people with his crisis rhetoric, Ronald Reagan finds himself presiding over an economic recovery, with the highest stock market averages in American history, even after the crash. But this recovery, however provident, is of a specially inflationary sort: it is not supported by either the rejuvenation of our failed industrial base or by a significant increase in productivity. Instead, the American economy is founded on permanent deficit spending, a disastrous imbalance of payments, and the need for a constant influx of imported capital. In a sense, then, the so-called recovery is born of nothing more substantial than the conviction that we ought to have one because, if we do not, a genuine crisis will follow.

As the president frequently, and crucially, reminds us, we have much to fear, but we must also give ourselves credit; and it is credit that has become the support of our recovery, in both the public and the private sectors. Just as the government finances its enterprises on borrowed money, the American consumer has followed the same strategy, with almost twenty percent of the average individual's disposable income now being generated by credit. If it were not for credit, there would be no recovery. Supply side or no supply side, if every dollar spent first had to be earned, there would be insufficient dollars to hire our recovery. At the same time, if there were no crisis, it is not likely that either people or governments would be prompted to spend so much money that they didn't have.

43

As it is, the longer we can keep our loans afloat, the better off we seem to be. Inflation breeds unreality, so that the sums represented by credit balances, while growing ever larger, become progressively less meaningful in terms of actual value, or in terms of their cumulative impact on consumer behavior. For example, it makes no sense these days to talk about "dollars" any more than a Bordeaux, except in terms of a particular year to identify which ones are being referred to, because some are clearly more valuable than others. And in any case, it is rarely the dollar price of goods or services that a person pays for; rather, it is merely the "interest" incurred by virtue of one's having been given credit: credit for the ability to desire things that others are willing to pay for; credit for maintaining a proper level of interest in the crisis that supports us all. The principal itself need never be repaid; and it is very much in the *public* interest that it should remain that way, which is why the government subsidizes the expansion of credit and penalizes the anachronistic use of cash. Within this environment, the representational economy of money and consuming falls apart, or else enters a nonreferential, "postmodern" phase.

Of course, under "normal" conditions, nobody would behave the way we do now. (Nor would we be able to do so ourselves unless we had inflation "under control.") Normally, people would spend less and save more, as they have always done, and as the residents of other developed countries without crises do. But these are *not* normal times, so we are not obliged to behave as if they were. In fact, it is our duty to do just the reverse. Insofar as present conditions are unprecedented, there can be no adequate preparation for them, which is what it means to have a crisis in the first place. Or more accurately, one cannot expect the past to offer a sufficient guide to what comes next, as John Naisbitt, for instance—among other futurologists—has made a fortune explaining in his best-seller *Megatrends:* "We have done the human thing: We are clinging to the known past in fear of the unknown future. . . . [But] those who are willing to handle the ambiguity of this in-between period and to anticipate the new era will be a quantum leap ahead of those who hold on to the past."[1] Experience is not enough; something additional will be called for if we are to move ahead; and that extra push is what crisis provides.

And that's where colleges and the humanities specifically come into the picture, as Americans struggle to transform a production-based economy into a newer, healthier, leaner one based on "information," or "service." The coverage of traditional representations is particularly consoling—however anachronistic it may have grown—when inflation has reduced so much of material life to depthless surfaces. As their name suggests, the humanities help people "do the human thing," but in such a way, one hopes, as will not interfere with their translation into a profitable, postindustrial future:

> The humanities have always been associated with the civic purpose of liberal education—to prepare the individual for making informed choices and acting responsibly. This purpose must be reasserted today, with a special urgency. As instant communications deluge us with information on social and political issues, we face civic choices more complex and perhaps more numerous than ever before. The humanities emphasize interpretation and criticism, indispensable techniques for participating in community life and keeping watch over its values.[2]

At this particularly anxious moment in our history, when people are understandably worried about making it into the next wave or credit cycle, they find themselves wanting (or so the story goes) the kind of centering experiences traditionally associated with the humanities, and none more so, perhaps, than the middle class, for whom education has always been a crucial element of identity. All too often, however, the schools, and their various faculties, are themselves unprepared, which is a point made by both the president and Secretary Bennett, among many other crisis custodians.

Whether the crisis is "real" or not is beside the point; the fact is that, for a great number of people, it *feels* real, and that feeling translates into new demands, new expectations, new (and profit-bearing) opportunities, and an unprecedented degree of attention presently being concentrated on the academy. Understandably, a great deal of discussion is being devoted to the definition, and the redefinition, of work. Paradoxically, it is the very fact that academics have never worked, in the usual sense of the term, that defines both their expertise and their vulnerability. They—we—can see the present situation more clearly than others precisely because we are outsiders, "disinterested" parties. At the same time, because history and the institutions we serve seem to have let us, perhaps unfairly, off the hook, we become the object first of envy, and then contempt.

Some of this is visited upon us from the outside, but a good deal of it is self-inflicted. Academics talk obsessively about crisis because they feel guilty; they tend to accept, and to reproduce—in seemingly endless studies and panel reports—the hard things they hear (or else imagine to be) said about them because they deserve to feel bad. After all, *we* don't have to work—not really—and *they* do;

and in times like these, things are getting pretty rough "out there."
This uneasy attitude is particularly characteristic of academics whose
field is the humanities because for them the difference between employment and "real life" is greater than with most other disciplines,
and along with it the susceptibility to self-doubt.

Geologists, mathematicians, even singers, can all function, they
can all "work" out there. But for a literature teacher, the only
alternative—professionally—to academia is unemployment; and
even the employment in question is often of dubious *real* value.
"What in God's name *is* the point of it all?" Philip Swallow asks in
David Lodge's novel *Small World,* only to be answered, immediately,
by the more seasoned and cynical theoretician, Morris Zapp:

> "There is no point . . . if by point you mean the hope of arriving at
> some certain truth. . . . The point, of course, is to uphold the institution
> of academic literary studies. We maintain our position in society by
> publicly performing a certain ritual, just like any other group of workers
> in the realm of discourse—lawyers, politicians, journalists. And as it
> looks as if we have done our duty for today, shall we all adjourn for a
> drink?"[3]

A friend of mine—a man more like Swallow than Zapp, as far as
professional self-confidence is concerned—occasionally mentions
the "fraud police," whom he expects to come knocking any moment
at his door. He holds out his wrists, as if waiting for the cuffs to be
snapped on. He'll go peaceably, he says, since he *knows* why they're
after him. It's a joke, of course, more or less. My friend is a full
professor, with tenure, still under forty; he's got a lot of articles, a
Guggenheim, plenty of respectful colleagues and enthusiastic students, and four books published. Insofar as the *real* work of the
profession is concerned, he's doing it very well, as everyone agrees,
which is why he has gotten to where he is. So why the fraud police?

I find his little joke unnerving every time I hear it because it
reproduces exactly the gesture—the proffered wrists of guilt—that
my favorite professor in graduate school used when he talked about
his version of the fraud police. He was a successful man too, like my
friend, though he seemed no better able to believe in his own success.
Other professions are prone to self-doubt, obviously. Literature
teachers are not the only ones given to night thoughts about being
exposed. But there's something that makes the guilt of the humanities
a more anxious burden. And I think it results from the failure of
professors to do work that nonprofessional adults can share in and
sympathize with. Patients may not understand medical jargon any

more than they can understand what their lawyer says to them about contracts, but they *can* understand the result of medical or legal practice: health, winning in court. By contrast, the result of professorial work is criticism, the thing that academics get rewarded for producing and that would largely appear nonsensical to a general reader, assuming that you could persuade him or her even to try reading it. Which means that Newman's communicable *idea* of a university is a lie, at least as far as the curators of language are concerned. Working inside that lie, at tasks that would be valued nowhere else, is what sets people listening, however jokingly, for the knock of the fraud police.

Sure, there are things you can *do* with a Ph.D. in Victorian literature—things other than teaching, that is—just like there are all sorts of wonderful things you can do with tofu. But nobody is ever fooled into thinking that the one is real food any more than the other is (or leads to) real work. In all the academic retraining manuals that I ever read, the first thing you get told about advanced degrees is that you ought to keep them to yourself if you decide to look for a regular job. "While you should not try to hide your education," the Modern Language Association itself even counsels, "you must play it down."[4]

I don't mean to imply that academic work is not as legitimate, or as tiring, as any other kind of work. What I am concerned with is the way in which people who do academic work are willing to talk about their activities, and in turn how those activities get interpreted by those outside the academy who are charged with the oversight of our institutions. Fundamental to the discourse of academic professionals is the distinction between real work and our work, between the real world and the academy. Given the present crisis, and the overdetermined role the academy has come to play in it, this distinction is enforced, on both sides, with a vehemence that is both unfortunate and potentially dangerous.

When teachers return from "vacation," for example, in order to begin the fall semester, they often ask each other, "Been getting any work done?" Or along about Thanksgiving, or spring break, when they feel particularly overburdened by committee assignments and grading, they complain that they have no time for their "work." In both instances the distinction between "work" and all the other things that go on in academic institutions might best be summarized as one between scholarship, which is real, and teaching, which is not. When academics talk about work, then, what they refer to invariably is writing, and especially writing intended for publication, either in articles (preferably articles accepted by "refereed" journals) or books (preferably ones published by a "good" publisher, which is to say, one as little "commercial" as possible). And it's no secret why this should be so. Work is what you get paid for doing, and writing is what academics get paid to do. That's how they get tenure, that's how they get raises, that's how they get promoted. That's how their "work" gets interpreted, in other words, by people outside their department—deans, provosts, presidents—who are in charge; and this is so because the people on the inside taught them the proper categories to apply. For example, according to a survey conducted by the American Council of Learned Societies, 70 percent of academics who began their careers since 1980 have already published at least one article in a refereed journal (the percentage is 88 for people in mid to late career); and close to half (47 percent) have already published their first book.[5] People who don't show up, or who teach badly, usually get fired sooner or later, of course. But they'd get fired a lot sooner if they didn't write, particularly now that the unacknowledged crisis of academic overproduction has made "qualified" people, which is to say ones willing to work hard, much easier to find. None of this is news, obviously.

Paradoxically, however, having once made this distinction between working and teaching, most academics are unwilling to treat their writing seriously, as if it were an authentic product. This reluctance drains the reality, retroactively, out of whatever activity, whatever "work," was required to produce it. (Not to mention the effect it has on the value of teaching, which is what keeps one from getting any *real* work done.) Referring to an article on George Eliot, for example, as if it had the same objective status, the same potential worth, as a loaf of bread or a Chevrolet (or even *Middlemarch* for that matter) sounds pretty romantic. It offends one's liberal sensibilities, the romanticism of which is probably best left unexamined— particularly now, when so many Americans are *out* of work. This ambivalence may account for the odd disposition of academic writing.

For a class of individuals so intent, necessarily, on getting into print, academics seem perversely afraid of being understood (which is a needless fear, given the minuscule readership of the average academic book or article). As to why this should be so, I think it has to do with the problem of work, and the effect that problem has on language: "Suppose a writer doesn't feel that he knows his readers, shares and defines their interests: or doesn't feel sure that he has any readers; or, even if he has, that he has them constantly. He would still write, but he would take account of the situation, and his style would reflect the account. One instance of a void or rift between himself and his readers would be enough to complicate his dealing with language."[6] One may agree or disagree with the charges Denis Donoghue makes against the "ferocious alphabets" of contemporary criticism, but his point about style remains a good one. Because they can't take work seriously, except as a void that separates them from other people, academics have nothing to share, nothing to put them in touch with their fellows, let alone the public at large. So they send out their anxious messages in bottles so tightly corked that only the few will ever become privy to their meaning. But at least the sender will be protected from the damning charge of "popularization" or "workmanlike" behavior.

However ill-conceived, this ambivalent conception of work, and particularly the distinction between working and teaching, remains fundamental to the present crisis. On the one hand, there are the academics, who respond to the demands of crisis—particularly demands that teachers begin to think more about what they do and why they do it—by discussing their "work," which is to say, the disauthenticated work of their writing and the "texts" (no longer called "works") on which that writing is based. On the other hand, there are the bureaucrats, politicians, and administrators, who are not particularly interested in the substance of scholarly articles and discussions but who are increasingly concerned with what does or doesn't go on in the classroom, and the role these goings-on could or should play in the present inflationary scenario. In neither case does one side seem to have anything particularly useful to say to the other. And when they do talk, the discussions are often conducted in the kind of inflationary clichés that get chiseled in stone over library doors but that have little or no practical value, the recent revival of crisis rhetoric offering an immediate case in point.

So what difference does that make, one might well ask? "Things, which can bear to be cut off from everything else and yet persist in living, must have life in themselves," as Cardinal Newman used to say. That so many of us are still here—gainfully employed, if not exactly working—just goes to show that he was right. There's plenty of vitality left in the university, and particularly in the liberal arts. And if the various panels and commissions are to be trusted, our importance in the future is likely to increase rather than diminish. The question, then, is not one of jobs. On that score, we have every reason to be optimistic.[7] The question is who is going to write our job descriptions. Or to put this another way, if we don't find some recognizable, real-world work to do, what sort of work is likely to be found for us?

In general, the public (and their officials) have already begun to examine the work of the teachers in their employ, and this is only to be expected. Given the present state of crisis, the value of education becomes greater, but so do the responsibilities of educators. As might be expected, the first target of the agenda for quality has been the public schools, where the non-substance of academic work has revealed itself immediately, since these teachers lack the symbolic achievements of publication to offer in their defense. They and their representatives are, however fortunately, the philosophical beneficiaries of America's higher education establishment; as such they have found themselves wholly without resources when required to make an account of their time. The case of certification exams has been particularly indicative. The reason to institute such exams, one assumes, is to insure uniform standards of quality. Doctors have exams, lawyers have exams, nurses have exams, even letter carriers have exams; and so should teachers, as the argument goes, in order to maintain high professional standards, which are especially important for a "nation at risk." What is significant is not the idea of the exams but the fact that the idea arose outside the teaching profession and has been accepted only slowly and grudgingly.

Whether such exams are a good or a bad thing is at issue. The point is that the teachers trained by America's colleges and universities have, unlike other professionals, been incapable of instituting an effective discourse with which to manage their own work, and by means of which they might account for that work to the general public. For example, in order to ensure that both he and his organization looked different from the rival National Education Association, Albert Shanker, of the American Federation of Teachers, made examinations into an issue. Now he has forced that issue on the NEA and its president, Mary Hatwood Futrell, who found herself without the means to oppose Shanker and his opportunistic politics of quality, which are not original with him but a clever borrowing from the repertory of crisis tropes that has recently become our national province.[8] The point, again, is not whether quality will be served by instituting some sort of national exam. The point is that the negative legacy of academic work has left teachers incapable of doing for themselves what others have now proved willing, and apparently able, to do for them.

Similarly, it comes as no surprise to find Shanker invoking the language, if not the specific presence, of Matthew Arnold and William

Bennett, the chief coreligionists of professional disinterestedness. "If we want a truly literate society," Mr. Shanker recently wrote in his weekly message in the Sunday *New York Times,* "the educational community has an obligation to transmit that society's long-standing culture—the sooner the better."[9] Or, as Secretary Bennett has said, "The humanities can contribute to an informed sense of community by enabling us to learn about and become participants in a common culture, shareholders in our civilization. . . . We should . . . want all students to know a common culture rooted in civilization's lasting vision, its highest shared ideals and aspirations."[10] This all sounds good, as it is supposed to do. But in a crisis such as ours, when some Americans suffer a great deal while others get rich, and when there is a pervasive feeling among the middle class that the only mobility they are likely to be offered is downward,[11] one begins to wonder what, if any, "culture" we can be said meaningfully to hold in common.

Perhaps the simplest, if not the least cynical, answer is *success.* For example, the same issue of the *Chronicle of Higher Education* that reported the findings of Bennett's panel also cited *In Search of Excellence* as the number one best-seller on American college campuses (28 November 1984, p. 2). That students should be concerned with the "lessons from America's best-run companies" comes as no surprise, given the goals that they espouse. With the freshman class of 1984 (92.6 percent of whom, by the way, had either met or exceeded the four years of English study recommended by the National Commission on Excellence in Education), 71.2 percent of those surveyed considered it either "essential or very important" to be "very well off financially."[12] For college students generally, the proportion is even greater (77 percent), suggesting that a yearning for the good life is one demonstrable effect of higher education, however embattled it has become. Understandably, then, three-quarters of all students say they are "worried about job prospects after college."[13]

To students who want to learn how to work, and work profitably if not necessarily well, one wonders how professors must look: people who disdain the quotidian idea of work in the first place; the same "professionals" who trained their high-school teachers, who in the arena of financial success and job prestige must be considered failures. Good work is work that pays, both monetarily and also in terms of respect. ("Becoming an authority in his or her field" was considered essential by 73.0 percent of those surveyed, 16 January 1985, p. 16.) Students understand this, and so, apparently, do their parents, whose representatives now demand that somebody—somebody from outside the academy, somebody who understands successful work—take charge of quality control. Insiders have shown themselves to lack both the initiative and the common sense.

This is precisely the point made by Governor Thomas Kean, of New Jersey, who wants to do for America's colleges and universities what Mr. Shanker and his colleagues propose to do for the public schools. Kean is chairman of the Education Commission of the States. In a report released two years ago, he proposed a comprehensive study of undergraduate education and the measures being taken by different states to improve quality, saying that such a project is called for "because concern about the quality of undergraduate education had not yet captured the public's attention to the same extent as concern about the quality of public schools."[14] There is notable here the same impulse toward consolidation and oversight that has saved from extinction the national Department of Education for Mr. Bennett to become secretary of. As one of Governor Kean's commission members remarked, "What happens to students is accidental rather than planned. . . . There is no cohesive program for students."[15] A year later the National Governors' Association has responded to this situation with their report, *Time for Results*: *The Governors' 1991 Report on Education,* which addresses both public and postsecondary education, and for the same reason: "Better schools mean better jobs. Unless states face these questions, Americans won't keep our high standard of living."[16]

The great vulnerability of academics, particularly those in the humanities, is that, on the one hand, they are being looked at with a closer scrutiny than ever before; and they are being expected to do more, or more kinds of things, than they should perhaps be expected to do. That is the burden placed upon them by crisis and by people's justifiable fear that things may be falling apart. As Secretary Bennett has pointed out, assurances of good intentions will no longer suffice—not in times such as these. Instead, standardized assessment and testing will be required because these measures offer "the surest way to turn the lofty statements of college catalogues into actual classroom practices."[17] Echoing the secretary's concern, the governors' report too is concerned with what works: "The problems in higher education have been documented by national reports and by key leaders from business, the military, and education itself. Despite this documentation, higher-education accrediting agencies apparently are unable to address the decline in academic standards and to hold member institutions accountable for their students' performance."[18] On the other hand, professors are not being allowed, nor are they allowing themselves, to take seriously the nature of their own work, with the result that they have nothing useful to say in response to the charges made against them. And even if they were willing to talk about what they really do, it's doubtful that officials or the public generally would consider scholarly publication an adequate response to questions about educational quality and student performance. Just as with the public schools, then, professors have proved incapable of disciplining themselves, which leads to calls for external assessment and oversight.

Paradoxically, there's no confusion, really, about what ought to be done, nor has there been for some years now. For instance, Donald Gray, the editor of *College English,* issued a general invitation in 1979 for readers of that journal to consider the relations between teaching and work, between the things we do and the intellectual and critical activities that we get paid for. Three years later, in 1982, he looked back on that invitation: "I have yet to read for CE (although I have read them in other journals) the essays I invited on the present status and function of literary history in the undergraduate curriculum, in the educations of high-school and college English teachers, and in our conceptions of who we are and what we do."[19] A glance at the tables of contents for the years subsequent to that statement will show that the future was to be no more fruitful than the past had been, which is regrettable, though perhaps understandable. Given the environment of skepticism and public scrutiny, members of the "profession" are uneasy just now about their "history," and the potentially dangerous associations that a too careful examination of history might occasion. If bad work has been done, after all, it won't pay to get too close to the people who did it. So nobody is particularly interested in making a common cause, at least not the sort that Donald Gray had in mind.

College English is the journal of the National Council of Teachers of English, a large professional organization that includes both college teachers and teachers who work in the public schools— people whose common bond, in other words, is that they all make their living by doing English. The fact that nobody submitted to Donald Gray the essays he was looking for, despite their having submitted such essays to other journals, is a result of this very fact; that is, the professional—as opposed to a literary or intellectual— character of his journal. It's one thing to talk about the practice of English in *Critical Inquiry,* say, which is published by the University of Chicago and includes contributions by such authorities as Jacques Derrida, Michel Foucault, and Wayne Booth, to name only three. It would be something quite different to write about working in a monthly such as *College English,* with its stapled spine, its obviously cheaper grade of paper, and its vaguely proletarian tone. In the first case, one might assume a certain anthropological distance, as if the matters being addressed had in fact come from somebody else's life. In the latter it would be clear that one worker was writing for an audience of other workers, in a journal where even things like writing workshops and classroom drills are common topics of discussion. And that is precisely the terrain of crisis. Given a choice, the members of our profession have preferred to keep separate the union hall and the drawing room.

This fact led Hazard Adams to the following patrician puzzlement, recorded in the pages of *Profession 83.* "It is a mystery to me," he wrote, "why we so often withhold from even our own majors systematic discussion of philosophical questions about our various subjects: What do we mean when we speak of literature? of language? Is there literature? About such questions we should have something to say. If we do not, we lose our sense of a purpose that can be explained and defended."[20] I expect we don't talk about these matters—least of all with our majors—for the same reason that parents are reluctant to tell their kids about the "facts of life." As an adult, one knows by definition what to do and needn't discuss it (or at least that used to be the case). Once bring the matter, the "facts," up with a kid, and the nature of relations changes in a fundamental and permanent way. Adulthood is suddenly demystified; its secret gets turned into some pretty simple procedures, which can be learned fairly quickly. And once the secret is out—the secret of how things work—the power of the adult is trivialized; it becomes mundane. Academics are no less traditionalists than parents used to be. They are in no hurry to reveal, for everybody to see, the "work" about which they may themselves feel a great deal of ambivalence, guilt, and anxiety. The result, as Adams says, is that we "lose our sense of a purpose that can be explained and defended." This is the precise loss to which Donald Gray's unheeded invitation gives testimony.

But as Gray said, academic work does get talked about—just as parents do have sex, even after the kids *know* what's going on. Such things must be done discretely, though, to preserve a proper decorum because there's more to growing up than just sharing knowledge. The "maturity" of the adolescent, just like Adams's common "purpose," has only a virtual reality. In practice, our community—like our "culture"—is rather more "ideological," as Trilling might say, than it is actual. The people who work in language, in other words, are the ones least willing, or able, to dispense with the internal distinctions that prevent us from talking, much less acting, as if we really held something in common. And crisis has done nothing to alleviate the tensions on which our class system is founded. Just the reverse, so there will be no overt discussion of work because it is by disguising the common basis of academic practice that the "profession" maintains its internal power structure.

As to the academic working class, the direct treatment of language (in writing courses) becomes an activity of "service," which has a lofty enough sound to it, though its status is more like that of other "service" jobs—working at a McDonald's, say, which is not a career, certainly, but acceptable for a person to do until he or she gets a "real" job. Robert Lyons has characterized the problematical status of the "writing teacher" in discussing the career of Mina Shaughnessy, who found herself recruited into a kind of work that, though necessary, was often discouraged—at least as a vocation for a serious professional: "For Shaughnessy, the experience must have reinforced a sense of being in the academy, but not of it. That anomalous position had been the mark of her earlier teaching career as well because she lacked the doctorate and had lived the precarious professional life of the part-time teacher. Such experiences made basic writing teachers generally see themselves, with justification, as a beleaguered lot."[21] Fortunately, things have changed a good deal since Mina Shaughnessy's first days at City College; many of the changes have to do with her own success and her having helped make "basic writing" an intellectually respectable undertaking. But history being what it is, teachers of writing have, predictably, been in no great hurry to embrace the other "traditional" side of a profession whose members have so happily, and for so long, condescended to those concerned with mere "comp."

The nonprofessional taint of that field is perhaps what has dissuaded the sort of serious speculation that Donald Gray kept looking for but failed to find. As he said, however, such speculating does go on; people do write about the nature of the "profession." But they don't do it in places like *College English,* thanks to what Paul Fussell might detect as certain "high prole" tendencies of that journal. The closer that academic practice, and the people who write about it, approach the quantifiable work of production, the less likely both are to be taken seriously as representative of the profession as a whole. As with any class system, the closer one gets to actual labor, the less likely one is to become the subject of official "history." It is no accident, then, that the work of writing instructors, which is generally administered by those with non-writing (which is to say "real") careers, should continue to be defined quantitatively, as if it were unknowable in any other way. A seasonally constituted labor force is contracted to teach so many students, assign so many papers, and in return get paid so much per credit hour (with periodic inspections by an administrative foreman to insure that employers are getting a fair day's work for a day's wage). In a pinch, practically any warm body will do, so the popular wisdom goes, provided there is close supervision.

This distinction between supervision and autonomy, between having a job and being a professional, is crucial—particularly now, when inflation has so undermined the reliability of mere dollars as an index of status. As Professor Fussell has pointed out in his book *Class,* "The degree to which your work is overseen by a superior suggests your real class more accurately than the amount you take home from it."[22] The important fact about writing, then, is that it is working class; and the important thing for the other members of the profession is that it should remain so. Otherwise, their own supervisory security might be in jeopardy. In a crisis environment, where work and the value of work are very much in question, and where credit can be counted on to take care of one's immediate material needs, what Pierre Bourdieu calls "symbolic capital" becomes at least as powerful as the genuine article.[23] For instance, at the school where I work/practice, I have a student who is a waiter in a Greek restaurant; he makes more money than some of the full professors in my department, and roughly twice the salary that I do. But the student "works," whereas neither I nor my colleagues do. His is a no-status job, whereas ours is prestigious, despite his making significantly more money than many of us. Work, in other words, belongs to the working class, whoever they may be, and however bright; and regardless of how much they get paid. At least, that has been the case traditionally.

But given our history of extended inflation and inflationary credit, the experience of *having* without *working* has become almost universally available, so that the representational significance of work, either negative or positive, gives way to a kind of ironic revaluation. Having less simply means having less. "Things" no longer stand for the time it took to "earn" them, and vice versa. It makes no more sense to work cheap, in other words, as the shabby genteel professor might (confident in the symbolic remuneration of cultural superiority), than it does to work too hard, as my student the waiter might, in absurd, unintentional parody of overachievement. Both forms of behavior represent anachronistic misapprehensions of

credit, which is now due, or at least obtainable, for practically everyone. In the larger space of the culture, then, the momentary, performative rituals of "life style" have supplanted the cumulative narrative of "character" as the basis of identity. This attitude of
inflationary populism places in jeopardy, of course, that symbolic
currency which constitutes the traditional capital (and power) of
academic careers. "Being a professor" no longer gets you very far,
in and of itself; instead, you need to demonstrate your professional
status actively—as Paul Fussell suggests—by making other people
work for you, whether directly or metaphorically. And that's what
the present crisis is all about—the preservation of symbolic capital,
the translation of class values into a new service-oriented environment. And that's why writing teachers, for example, must continue
to work: so that others, by differing from them, may remain professionals. That these teachers have often made a virtue of necessity is
admirable. That the nature of our common work remains undiscussed
is not.

The entry of the present educational crisis into the public
schools offers a case in point. Here the agenda for quality has arrived
at a particularly inopportune moment because there are too few
teachers rather than too many, the symbolic remuneration for such
work being just about as skimpy—and therefore as attractive—as
the actual wages. So the drive to start weeding people out has been
hampered by there being too few people to begin with. In states such
as California and Texas, where population growth has made the need
for new teachers immediate, the crisis has proved especially frustrating, but also revealing. These states, along with Virginia and New
Jersey, have devised alternative plans for certifying new teachers
that absolve them of taking college education courses. The National
Education Association, among other organizations, has objected
strongly to such plans. At issue is the nature of the teacher's job, and
the kind of training necessary to prepare a person for that job. If
teachers are professionals, then presumably they don't need education courses, any more than doctors, or lawyers, or college professors
do. If they are not, then presumably they do. In the latter case,
education departments will survive and prosper; in the former, they
will probably cease to exist. So just as literature professors preserve
their status by banishing their composition colleagues to the nether
reaches of work, education professionals have now found it necessary to de-professionalize the careers of their students and, more
recently, large numbers of their colleagues as well.

At present this aspect of the crisis remains unresolved, though

still indicative, particularly as regards public feeling about the state
of our schools. As far as such feeling is concerned, the crisis in
education is ending, if it is not already over. The Gallup organization
found (in their seventeenth annual poll of attitudes toward education)
that 71 percent of those surveyed gave their neighborhood school a
grade of A or B. Only 7 percent rated their schools D or F. These
findings represent the strongest showing of confidence in the schools
since the palmy, pre-crisis days of 1976.[24] More than anything else,
then, the "crisis," like the "recovery" that produced it, seems to
refer to nothing more substantial than the *idea* of crisis. Thus far
there has been no time for fundamental changes in the conditions
that engendered the crisis; yet the mere fact of its having been talked
about, by the right kinds of people, appears to be solution enough.
As Governor Thomas Kean, of New Jersey, recently remarked,
"education is now good politics."[25] For instance, the issue of com-
petency testing has generated a good deal of controversy, not to
mention political capital. One can assume, therefore, that the matter
is being looked after. What hasn't gotten much coverage is the results
of those tests—probably because they demonstrate the practical
valuelessness of such tests in the first place, at least as presently
conceived. Two years ago in New Jersey, for example, 90 percent of
teacher training–program graduates passed the tests, with scores of
better than 95 percent for those entering teaching by some alternate
route.[26] Any test which that many people pass is no test at all. Of
course, if very many people failed the tests, America would run out
of teachers, and nobody wants that to happen.

But then, these tests, like the "professional" discourse of which
they are the product, have almost nothing to do with incoming teachers, and a great deal to do with teachers who already have, and wish
to keep, their jobs. In this instance a group of academic employees—
education professors—found themselves confronting a genuine crisis: one produced by falling enrollments and a challenge by external
agents to assume management responsibilities. Instead of giving up,
they did what academics tend to do: they found a relatively powerless
group, their students, on whom to project the onus of "work."
That—the working-class status of others—is the symbolic capital
yielded by the present crisis. Simultaneously, those—the professors—who have made this fortuitous discovery are in a position to
benefit from its symbolic profits.

However, the mere imposition of tests is a relatively crude
response to external, political challenge. Subsequently, the "Holmes
Group" (a consortium of education-school deans and professors) has

developed a much more sophisticated response to the charge that the academic establishment is incapable of training the teachers that America needs if we are to be "a nation prepared." They, like the Carnegie Forum on Education and the Economy (a group of politicians and management personnel), have insisted on the professionalization of public-school teaching.[27] In order to achieve this entirely admirable goal, they have assumed a managerial role with regard to the present education establishment. Undergraduate degrees in education will no longer be offered in schools that submit to Holmes evaluation or that adopt the Carnegie plan, which means the installation of a two-tier class system such as exists already in English departments, where some people are professionals (either by virtue of managerial or scholarly achievements) and others are mere service-providers, charged with the work of "comp." The members of that working class will now be joined by recently de-professionalized members of education departments, who no longer have a subject but merely a useful service to provide. Thus, typically, an endangered group—or part of it—has escaped falling into the working class by sending somebody else there instead.

I don't mean to imply that this ought not to happen necessarily, or that the proposed changes won't produce better schools. In any event, both the Carnegie and Holmes plans promise good business for liberal arts departments, which would gain significant enrollment if the proposals are implemented because students would major in specific subject areas rather than simply adding a few courses to their education major as presently happens. And in the mind of the public, for whom the crisis in the schools is over anyhow, as a matter of news coverage, the academic profession has probably gained—selectively—in prominence and authority. This attitude makes it questionable, however, whether this same public will decide to spend the estimated $50 billion that it might cost to implement a plan such as the Carnegie Forum's.[28] Either way, "we" have won. The problem is the way in which academic professionals have gone about winning. We have responded to, and escaped, the present crisis by taking charge of it, by becoming its executors. But at a moment when the culture as a whole, no less than the academic profession, is undergoing a fundamental redefinition of work, we may be doing ourselves no favors by turning work into somebody else's problem. In the short term, this may seem attractive, and even profitable. In the long term, however, the capital that we produce may turn out to be valueless, and our profession along with it.

The difficulty is that academic professionals have yet to develop a coherent notion of work, except as something that *other* people do. The potentially dangerous results of this projection can be illustrated clearly enough using literature departments as an example. On the one hand, there is certainly a lot of work to be done, even more than there used to be, now that the basics are again in vogue. On the other, once it becomes possible to define teaching as a form of work, then there's no longer any point in paying professionals to do it, either directly or in supervisory roles. A centralized administration (already in place) could accomplish such tasks much more efficiently. After all, that's their job, their *work*. Also, contracted employees are vastly more cost-effective than permanent ones, which is a primary lesson of the service revolution. Given that fact, most colleges and universities have seen a significant increase in "adjunct" lines, as compared with tenure-track appointments, particularly in such crisis-driven areas as English.[29] In my own department, for example, which appears to be statistically typical of large state universities, 34 percent of the sections of required courses are taught by full-time tenured or tenure-track faculty; the remaining 66 percent are taught by part-time or contracted employees—workers, in other words.

That's why we find ourselves in the present contradictory situation, which combines a conservative return to tradition (the "re-claiming of a legacy," as Secretary Bennett has called it) with an attack on the very agents usually associated with preserving that tradition: not just the professors, but such things as tenure and job security that we think of as essential to what we do. Ours is a crisis not of content, then, but of practice; the discussions that matter, which is to say the ones involving money and changes in the law, are centered not on the nature of canon but on the organization of people's work lives. But it is precisely that topic—the canon, either for or against—that usually defines our notion of ourselves as professionals, and understandably so, since it remains the basis of both syllabi and professional writing. And in any case, since we have imposed upon others the burden of work, all we are left with is an elegant, canonical superfluity.

Two recent issues of *Critical Inquiry* offer an illustrative case in point. They contain the sorts of essays that Donald Gray was presumably referring to when he invited, but failed to receive, considerations of "who we are and what we do," though the views of his editorial constituents might differ from the ones expressed. The September number for 1983 (vol. 10) was devoted to the discussion of literary "canons." The eight men and one woman who contributed essays—two of them holders of endowed chairs—are respected, and representative, members of their profession. Theirs is the success that the rest of us aspire to. What they undertook, they did very well, as might be expected: they wrote about the texts and the critical theories that constitute the field of academic literature, the domain of "real" work. What they did not do is relate that work, and by extension their profession, to the larger field of academic work in general, which is only to be expected. To have done so would dissolve the very differences on which their status and that of their institutions depend, schools such as Pennsylvania, Princeton, Yale, and Berkeley. These are "classy" places, as Professor Fussell would doubtless recognize, his current employer being among them. As such, they must remain symbolically separated from work, which is the point of such supervisory performances as the one enacted in the *Critical Inquiry* special issue.

Despite the understandable self-confidence of the contributors to the special issue, there's a certain dubiousness about the whole undertaking, and its relevance to the crisis that it implicitly, if not actually, addresses. This dubiousness has to do with a problem implied in a somewhat earlier special issue (September 1982), which was devoted to "The Politics of Interpretation." Of the theorists consulted, very few thought that their "work" had any relevance to an undergraduate curriculum, which is the part of the curriculum where most people employed by the humanities in general and literature in particular still find their careers. The theoretical instruments of self-consciousness, in other words, are deemed to be inappropriate except for specialized audiences of graduate students and fellow professionals. By definition, then, the work of literary criticism, which is to say the "real" work by which people's careers are judged and rewarded, takes on a highly ambiguous character as regards one's life as a teacher. Given the view of the experts, the general run of professorial practice could hardly aspire to rise above an astute superfluity, which is what makes work such a touchy subject to begin with.

But the problems don't stop here. Whatever the role of theory in the undergraduate curriculum, both its prominence and its dissemination among college teachers is unprecedented; and thanks to the generosity of the NEH and their summer programs, it is being introduced to high-school instructors as well. As to whether or not the average teacher will ever become a theoretician, that's up to him or her to decide. The point is that the job of literature has become inescapably theoretical and necessarily self-conscious, which is a good thing potentially. The days are gone forever when a person could think (let alone write) as if texts "speak for themselves," thereby disguising as a ventriloquized, natural voice the particular, cultural bias and/or ignorance of the teacher. Once divested of our natural innocence, it's not as if our job has gotten any easier though.

On the contrary, self-consciousness seems more a burden than a blessing, particularly now, when crisis demands that teachers administer a traditional canon that, so far as their professional lives are concerned, everyone has long since ceased to believe in. As Robert von Hallberg, who was the editor of the special issue on canons, has pointed out, "Though the subject of canon-formation is addressed now only with irony, it might be thought of as the traditional dream of ambitious critics."[30] Thus the double bind of the practicing professional who is bound to the traditional dreams of humanistic studies (and who is reminded assiduously of these by ambitious public servants and academic, crisis politicians), but who would get laughed out of town—and out of print—if he or she took them seriously. By maintaining our present "ideological" position as regards the otherness of work and the ironic value of canonical "culture," we remain absent from the site of social transformation and withhold from it whatever critical intelligence we have at our disposal. At this juncture there is nothing inherently wrong with theory, in other words. Just the reverse. But the ambiguous nature of our work tends to dissipate the potentially crucial application of theory to our institutional situation. "The particular mission of the humanities," as Edward Said has argued, "is, in the aggregate, to represent *noninterference* in the affairs of the everyday world."[31] It is not my point, necessarily, to argue for or against this "mission." That the mission goes forward unattended, however, with nobody apparently responsible either for its conduct or its results is a failing both dangerous and reprehensible—a failing that leads some, not surprisingly, to thoughts of the fraud police.

3. History

$\mathbf{T}$he university is a representational institution, and has been so since the nineteenth century, when middle-class needs turned it into one: it represents a culturally privileged solution to that inflationary crisis which is the necessary precondition for a modern industrial society. As the economies of first England and then the United States shifted from agriculture to production, it became necessary to produce individuals capable of comprehending, and subsequently reproducing, the relations necessary to sustain such a transformation. But in order for such a transformation to occur in the first place, there had to be an inflationary introduction of possibility; there had to be too many choices before the historical patterns of the past could be seen as arbitrary, and therefore subject to conscious alteration:

> Scarcely any one, in the more educated classes, seems to have any opinions, or to place any real faith in those which he professes to have. . . . It requires in these times much more intellect to marshal so much greater a stock of ideas and observations. This has not yet been done, or has been done only by very few: and hence the multitude of thoughts only breeds increase of uncertainty. Those who should be the guides of the rest, see too many sides to every question. They hear so much said, or find that so much can be said, about everything, that they feel no assurance of the truth of anything.[1]

Thus the inflationary reflections of John Stuart Mill in a diary entry for 13 January 1854. Within such an environment—as we have long since come to understand—the effect is to devalue actual memories and habits of thought, or at least to deprive these of "natural" authority, and to replace such fixity with the "historical" consciousness that nature might assume any number of possible shapes, the determination of "truth" being more a pragmatic than a metaphysical question.

This change was crucial for the "more educated classes" in particular if they were to provide the managerial apparatus for a developing, bureaucratic state. The "individual," then, ceases to be a matter of unconscious assumption and becomes instead an object of intentional choice, or production. And given the inflationary circumstances, wherein "the multitude of thoughts only breeds increase of uncertainty," freedom of choice creates the need for institutional representations of right and wrong choosing, since, as Mill wrote, "it requires in these times much more intellect to marshall so much greater a stock of ideas and observations." Institutions come to represent—by the collective assembly of various "faculties"—the resources necessary for a successful, individual life. But because of the complexity of the situation, no individual can be as "smart" as the institution, so that such representations—of the law, the university, the government—become *virtual* rather than literal, which is the source of their power. There is always more to the representation than any one person can master, so that the "truth" of things becomes a bureaucratic rather than a personal experience.

As it emerges, then, the role of the modern university is to represent an imaginary solution by which this inflationary environment could be submitted to individual management, and in such a way as to yield the general, social profit of order and the personal benefit of "improvement." "We want an authority, and we find nothing but jealous classes, checks, and a deadlock," as Matthew Arnold wrote in *Culture and Anarchy*; "culture suggests the idea of *the State*. We find no basis for a firm State-power in our ordinary selves; culture suggests one to us in our *best self*."[2] The function of the university, then, was to represent the economy of best selves: it assembled the faculties required on an individual basis; and it instituted a larger domain—a "culture"—within which their several efforts might assume a productive, social relevance. In this way the university produced a symbolic solution to historical and material conflict. In place of the anarchic crisis confronting the State—the deadlock of class conflict and potential warfare—it offered a classless model of Culture in which, and for which, people of all kinds might work meaningfully together.

In this sense the university exists more as *idea* than reality: its role is "symbolic," as Bourdieu might say, since culture is realized only for those few who actually join the faculty; and even the elect remain, at most, partial representatives of a greater than individual whole. For the rest, even though they do not become members of the university, or even attend, they are no less able to participate in the symbolic economy represented by the institution and the ideal of "education" for which it stands. As Tulliver, the benighted miller, explains in George Eliot's *The Mill on the Floss,* regarding the plans he has for his son Tom, " 'You see, I've made up my mind not to bring Tom up to my own business. . . . I want to give him an eddi-cation as he'll be even wi' the lawyers and folks, and put me up to a notion now an' then.' "[3] Sustained by a belief in the transformative powers of "eddication," more than one Victorian father would share Tulliver's dream (and submit to a life of hard work to achieve it): the dream that his son wouldn't follow him in "business" but rise above the father's state to become the equal of "lawyers and folks." And in a sufficient number of representative cases, the dream was real-ized, so that the "idea" of education—however clearly understood—become a standard feature of middle-class "culture."

Just like the virtual representation of electoral politics, then, the virtual accessibility of the university—or, as in Tulliver's case, its tutorial representatives—becomes a substitute for actual democ-racy. It offers *potential* access to the instruments of privilege and control and extends the ultimate promise of individualist democracy that you can make whatever you want of yourself, the only limits being perseverance and native ability (and not incidentally the pres-ervation of the structure that produces the goods being offered, including the serviceable "self" on which economy depends). As demands are placed upon a culture, then, to open itself to broader participation, the university offers a powerful simulacrum response. Everyone need not be admitted; but representative individuals are, and their stories are made known. Thus, exclusivity gives way to "improvement."

If the university is to continue in this transformative role, how-ever, its centrality must be maintained, for which purpose the insti-tution alone is not sufficient. The functioning of the university de-pends on a convergence of discourses that originate both internally and externally, so as to confirm the symbolic economy represented by the institution. That was understood clearly enough by Victorian public officials like Arnold, who was a school inspector, just as it is understood by our own secretary of education. The university, or the educational ideal that it symbolizes, must be the acknowledged *answer* to a *question* that is generally shared, and widely reproduced. The power of institutional representation depends as much upon Mr. Tulliver's belief, in other words, as it does upon the demonstrable culture of its graduates. For that matter, it is probably easier to believe in a *virtual* good, such as that represented by education or representative government, than it is to remain faithful once you are in actual possession. In any case, education, except of the most rudimentary sort, has remained a minority achievement, so that aspirants have vastly outnumbered the residents of culture. And even for the "educated classes," knowledge rarely served as its own end, despite what Cardinal Newman may have thought. On the contrary, knowledge—culture—remained desirable because it got you around in the world.

In that connection the most important feature of Arnold's university is that it worked. The language of "culture" was immediately (however self-consciously) practical. It accomplished a crucial task for the middle class, who found themselves in need of an idiom, an ideology, with which to economize their social and political identity, and with which to remove from that identity—as from their money— the taint of having been recently "made." The university worked because it taught people who went there—or who participated vicariously in its social forms—how to represent their relations both to each other and to the conditions responsible for their arrival "in the world." It lent them the weight of a cultural tradition by which the "individual" might escape the irrelevance of recent creation. In this context Arnold understood his ideological business far better than his perennial adversary Thomas Huxley did. For the latter it was a disgrace that "university training shuts out of the minds of those subjected to it, the prospect that there is anything in the world for which they are specially fitted."[4] Of course, that was the precise point of a middle-class father's (or later a working-class father's) sending his son to school: so as to unfit him, both by training and expectation, for the *idea* of work, regardless of what his actual career might end up being.

For that purpose Huxley's practical notion of education was irrelevant. The "great expectations" of Charles Dickens's Pip, for example, are paradigmatic. " 'I have been bred to no calling, and I am fit for nothing,' " he explains to his friend Herbert, which is, of course, precisely the intention of his benefactor, Abel Magwitch, who vicariously solaces his own frustrations by buying himself a gentleman.[5] " 'In every single thing I went for, I went for you,' "

Magwitch explains to Pip; " 'It was a recompense to me, look'ee here, to know in secret that I was making a gentleman' " (p. 339). The old convict's life comes to significance by virtue of referring to the culturally scripted production he has paid for: the production of a gentleman. And once having achieved his goal, Magwitch knows that he must see to it that the actual past is never spoken because to do so would deprive Pip of the status that his acquired culture represents: " 'I ain't made Pip a gentleman . . . not fur me not to know what's due. . . . Muzzled I have been . . . muzzled I am at the present time, muzzled I ever will be' " (p. 355).

Pip's situation is particularly difficult because his transformation has been effected outside the university. There is no institution, therefore, to mediate between memory and culture, to assume the symbolic role of alma mater in place of the actual parental figures whom his expectations have forced him to abandon. Therefore, Pip must confront his past directly, personally, and by surprise, which becomes the source of Dickens's plot. For the majority of aspirants to culture, however, the university provided a much smoother, if less dramatic, agency, just as it has offered a simpler—and more publicly exploitable—vehicle of vicarious philanthropic endowment.

As the English historian George Kitson Clark has pointed out, the university emerges in its modern role of credentialing agent concurrent with the rise of the middle class:

> Some tests were needed which would extend the number of gentlemen, and which would rationalize and moralize the conception of a gentleman for a generation which the old naive touchstones of blood, or heraldry, or landownership would by no means suffice. One obvious test that came to be of increasing importance was the test of education. . . . It came to be increasingly assumed that a gentleman would have had the education of a gentleman, a proposition which in time might carry the convenient converse that someone who had had the education of a gentleman was likely to be a gentleman. It was a conception that was going to be of very great importance in the nineteenth century and its development and consolidation was much assisted by the fact that an increasing number of people were receiving what could be considered the education of a gentleman.[6]

Given this new ideological mission, the growth of the university would be closely tied to the arrival of the middle class, whose needs it came increasingly to represent. After a century of declining enrollments, both Oxford and Cambridge began to grow in size about 1800, this growth reaching a peak in the third quarter of the century, when the size of the freshman class at Cambridge, for example, increased in number by 200 percent (p. 256). This growth corresponds with the well-documented shift in population away from the country and toward cities, away from agriculture and toward forms of employment based on capital and the kinds of upward mobility for which culture, rather than vocational skill, was required.

Between the first (1832) and the third (1884) Parliamentary Reform Bills, when the growth of the university became quite rapid, vocations associated with the middle class were expanding at a rate much faster than that of the general population. During this period, for example, the general population increased 182 percent, with the population of London growing at roughly the same rate (190 percent). Meanwhile, employment in professional positions increased by 253 percent, with public administration increasing by 365 percent.[7] More than ever before, there were large numbers of people living in conditions of relative affluence in a place—the city—where they had no history, and where actual memory, such as Pip's memory of the forge, might in fact inhibit their reasonable "expectations": people who now made their way among "lawyers and folks" that Mr. Tulliver could only guess at. In this context the virtual past of "culture," and the status conferred by an institutional warrant of gentility, became highly desirable to a class whose claim to social participation was necessarily based on what it could imagine, rather than who it had been. Arnold's discourse—the still powerful discourse of culture—is the product of ideological necessity, and it would find an equally attentive audience in the United States, although our need of culture was somewhat delayed, and also more diffuse, because of a number of factors, the Civil War and western expansion being among them.[8]

Nevertheless, in this country, as in his own, Arnold's ideal worked, and with such unexpected success that instead of undergoing proletarian revolutions, such as Marx anticipated, England and America gave rise to a growing, and increasingly stable, middle class. Arnold, of course, made much of the necessary "disinterestedness" of the liberal arts, as did Cardinal Newman. This claim, in other words, constituted a recognized value of universal knowledge; and for that matter, it still does, as evidenced by Secretary Bennett's demand that teaching rise above mere "ideology." Having achieved a place in the world by getting over history, the executors of culture are not anxious to reenter it, or to grant it an institutional voice. Better to keep "muzzled" as Magwitch well understood. But in fact, the university functioned because it *was* interested, and in a specifically historical way, as Kitson Clark points out: it became the place where the compromises of middle-class life got worked out; institutionally, it represented a way into the culture for people who were willing to work.

The success of this enterprise can be judged by its having not only averted such revolutionary violence as took place in France or Germany, for example, but by its having produced an empire on which the sun never set (thanks largely to the service, and material resources, of a properly trained middle class). Similarly, the education received "at university," whether virtual or actual, was so good that the newly emergent class did not undertake the democratizing social revolution, which ideologues of the establishment such as Thomas Carlyle feared almost as much as a violent overthrow of government. Instead, the newly enfranchised preferred to reproduce, if not actually to reelect, those whose traditions they had now come— "virtually"—to share, so that the great "Victorian compromise" yields not a republic but Princess Di.

In this context the university is perhaps best thought of as space rather than content—a space created by the intersection of crisis and desire. This space, then, models the larger, social space; or rather, it models a certain ideal of that space. For instance, toward the end of his life, William Makepeace Thackeray made the following pronouncement at a dinner in Edinburgh, given in his honor: "I belong to the class that I see round me here, the class of lawyers and merchants and scholars, of men who are striving on in the world, of men of the educated middle classes of this country. And belonging to them my sympathies and my desires are with them."[9] Thackeray was born into a family of Yorkshire yeomen and educated at Trinity College, Cambridge. Institutionally, then, he had acquired the *virtue* of culture by means of which he discovered a new affiliation with the heretofore nonexistent "class" that he saw around him at dinner: "lawyers and merchants and scholars . . . men . . . striving on in the world." It would have been impossible for the educational institutions of Victorian society to consolidate such historically different groups and give them a common class identity—a meaningful "role"—unless the space of the university had accurately represented the virtual desire of an external constituency to belong to something in common; and unless the inflationary domain of social possibility had afforded the degree of mobility required for its accomplishment.

As I suggested, if the distinguishing feature of this compromise is its having worked, the distinguishing feature of contemporary universities is their failure to do so—and for largely historical reasons. In a society based on growth and individual mobility, there can be no permanence, no fixity. The only fixed aspect of life is the necessarily renewable crisis of choice. That much has been the same since John Stuart Mill lamented the overwhelming "stock of ideas and observations." That effect, that *press* of external possibility, is what constitutes the distinctive character of modern life. But as modern gives way to postmodern, Mill's statement becomes impossible. Not that the same inflationary conditions don't still prevail because they do. If anything, the proliferation of possibility is vastly greater now, particularly as enforced by the agents of media coverage.

But it would not occur to anyone nowadays to pose inflation as a question, as Mill did—particularly not a question to be answered by the institutional representation of culture:

> The superannuation of the past, the fluidity of personal relations, the malleability of the physical environment before technology and of the spiritual environment before the mythmaking of advertising, journalism, entertainment, and political propaganda combine not only to erode our assurance of reality but our ability to recognize the erosion and see it as harmful. Alienation from work, from the possibility of community, from belief in the possible intelligibility of experience have increasingly become the shared ground of middle-class life.[10]

Thus the familiar characterization—in this case from Gerald Graff— of postmodern life, the postmodern "moment" being, of course, one confined almost exclusively to the class whose identity has traditionally been bound to the university. If *culture* represented the institutionalized habit of "right" choice, such choosing has become superfluous as a feature of either individual or social identity. A unitary culture has given way to momentary and disjunctive *situations*— office, disco, gymn, bedroom, and so on—each with its own impermanent codes, so that institutions such as the university, with its presumption to general knowledge and classic fixity, have grown too slow and ill-adapted to be useful: alma mater becomes ideological dinosaur. And in any case, the value of culture as a means of mobility has long since become questionable in a society such as ours, where it's easy to get credit for being middle-class, regardless of who you are or whether or not you went to school. Culture has nothing further to offer—at least in a traditional sense—when class ceases to function as a meaningful social difference.

This change in conditions has brought a consequent change in institutional representations. Whereas Arnold's institution modeled a social consolidation—a desirable end to narrative crisis—ours models a post-narrative experience of superfluity: "alienation from work, from the possibility of community, from belief in the possible intelligibility of experience." Or, to put this another way, the university has lost its *virtue*; it has become undesirable to the class of "strangers" upon whose kindness, and imaginative investment, its symbolic worth depended. And for good reason. The model of *production*, whether of automobiles or of culture, is no longer a sufficient representation of what sustains the lives, or the expectations, of most Americans. Only two out of every ten workers today is employed in the traditional way; seven out of ten are now occupied with the insubstantial errands of "service."[11] Most people, in other words, no longer make anything real; there are no tangible products that might stand, cumulatively, for the meaning of the labor that has produced them. Similarly, the model of production, or the escape from its effects, no longer represents a meaningful social agenda.

The "educated," of course, have almost always been service providers; they were the managers, for example, who made the empire run. But the thing they managed, and the truths through which they consolidated their managerial position, are all ultimately formulated on the expectation of meaningful production and accumulation. That's what it meant to institute a culture in Arnold's formulation: "to make the best that has been thought and known in the world current everywhere" (p. 426): to manage efficiently, in other words, a system of production and distribution that applied to the whole of the society (despite obvious disparities in the apportioning of its goods and services). However, such an economy of expectation no longer finds fulfillment in actual experience; Arnold's agenda has gone the same way as the open hearth furnace. This change, coupled with the vastly greater number of jobs that the university is expected to provide training for (along with the level of technical skill required in each), has made especially complex the problem of economizing an effective, postmodern "culture."

Yet the university enforces with new vigor—now that "crisis" is upon us—the same narrative agenda that Arnold and Newman invented. This is truer of American institutions than English ones. Here educational time is no less carefully plotted than factory life used to be, for both students and faculty. Each school year is broken down into separate acts, whether semesters or quarters; and every student is cast in a role appropriate to her/his progress: freshman, sophomore, junior, senior, and so on. For the faculty the narrative calendar is the same, except that in place of student roles, there are

professorial ones: assistant, associate, full, with the additions of
tenure and endowed chairs adding further plotting options. This production-based agenda is, in fact, an American invention that dates
from the nineteenth century.[12]

In order to get over its past, the middle class endowed—both
materially and imaginatively—the narrative institution of the university. Having given historical difference up to institutional curation,
they were free to enter "the culture." So pervasive has education
become in this country that we no longer require narrative institutions
to help us get over the past. Collectively, we've long since forgotten
all about it, which is why class no longer says anything meaningful
about our society.

The contemporary rhetoric of crisis merely renews the academic franchise upon an economy of desire that has already become
anachronistic. The reimposition of "discipline," "coherence,"
"standards," and so forth, merely refurbishes an irrelevant structure
that now survives as a hollow, unrepresentative relic. As a result,
many people—both inside and outside the university—find themselves in jobs they can't "imagine"; or else they are deprived of
work altogether and are without resources to figure out what has
gone wrong, which explains the popularity of a figure such as Bruce
Springsteen, for example. Just as he claims, most of his adolescent
fans were "born in America," only to find that experience—and the
history accompanying it—an inadequate guide to their situation. The
institutions of the culture have failed; they no longer represent what
is "really" going on, or prepare people for it. Thus Springsteen's
nostalgia for the intelligible, if cliché, forms of blue-collar life, the
power of which consists in absence: from their having been displaced
by a supposedly incomprehensible present. The problem, however,
is not so much with work, or the present, as it is with those imaginary
forms by means of which people account for their relation to work.
For example, when it was actually possible to live the life of production, the majority of American workers aspired to something better,
if not for themselves, at least for "the kids." And the university
helped them get it. Now that life is gone, and with it the virtue of the
narrative institutions it gave rise to.

The nature of work has changed, with narrative forms no longer
offering a sufficient guide to the life of information/service; but there
has been no concurrent change in the imaginary economy of culture,
which leaves people stranded, without anything to belong to except
the past, about which they know very little except for what the
"media" tell them.

Given the enforced cruelties of our present economic transformation, the urge for abdication, for "disinterest," is perhaps understandable, like the popularity of Springsteen. But that makes no easier the task of comprehending the role of the university. What it does do, however, is illustrate the character of academic "intelligence." Having renounced the grand signified of *culture,* academics do not necessarily relinquish their presumptive claim to universal knowledge, for which purpose irony and cynicism serve as well as belief. *We* still know what everyone else is all about, regardless of the intellectual disarray that the academy collectively represents. And *we* still control the specialized credentials that people need. Crisis brings us hostages who are going to have to take liberal arts classes, like it or not, once they show up here. And best of all, they are still showing up. In fact, the nature of info-serv training is such that an estimated 2–3 percent of the work force will likely have to retrain every year (regardless of what happens to other sources of enrollment), so that business is only going to get better.[13]

What such clients are likely to encounter once they arrive is a predatory fragmentation. Set upon by various contending faculties, their *situation*—least of all their situation in relation to work—cannot be economized by the available resources of the institution: "The abundance of reports diagnosing and prescribing for our schools and colleges, the urgency with which they are argued, the evidence that they summon, and the analyses that they offer are persuasive evidence that there is a profound crisis."[14] True enough, as per the findings of the American Association of Colleges. The only surprise is that these people were surprised to have been scooped. "When our committee was formed in 1982," their report reads, "we feared that our eventual report would be a voice crying in the wilderness. We now know that we have joined a chorus" (p. 12). As it turns out, crisis has replaced culture as the referent of academic representation; crisis organizes the academy as culture can no longer usefully do, so that the university becomes an essential site for the ideological meltdown of the middle class. The narratively administered individual is led through a rhetorically if not literally upgraded program, which ends in spontaneous deconstruction: the forced realization that there is no "life" represented here, whether one based on work or something else; nor is there any means of accounting for what is absent, since the medium of our common discourse has long since ceased to refer to anything except its own various, contentious addresses.

4. Language

By now the transformation of the university, particularly the American university, into exactly the sort of "practical" institution that Huxley advocated and Arnold deplored has long since been accomplished, with the consequent relegation of the liberal arts to the "peripheral" position that they currently occupy. Yet people—both inside and outside the academy—persist in talking as if Arnold had won the debate rather than having so conspicuously lost it. More often than not, academics who work in the liberal arts still think, speak, and write as if they represented "the culture," however "deconstructed" their idea of that, or any other signified, may have become. This illusion is not entirely without basis, however, because when outsiders such as Secretary Bennett wish to discuss the connection between the university and the wider life of the society, they don't address the institution piecemeal, as a business or bureaucratic structure. They rarely talk specifically of its more affluent or relevant departments; rather, they talk about the liberal arts. At any rate, they use the language of culture native to the liberal arts, and they apply it as if that were still the idiom appropriate to the academic representations in general. Given this state of affairs, it's possible to say that, despite real evidence to the contrary, whatever happens to the liberal arts happens to the "university." Or to put this another way, the university has become a problem of language peculiar to the liberal arts.

And these days the most immediate feature of this language problem is the figure of crisis, which represents the defining event of late American life. Given the economy of academic production, and the admittedly marginal position of the humanities, crisis only hastens the results that many of its sponsors ostensibly seek to prevent. Rather than arresting internal divisions, it merely accelerates their development, though in sublimated form, such as the "profession-alization" of writing, which de facto amounts to the de-profession-alization of language teaching. Similarly, the return to "standards," or "basics," merely exposes *culture*, to ever larger audiences, as a textual anachronism, now wholly deprived of market value or insti-tutional reference. For all the talk of tradition and the reclaiming of past legacies, then, the two immediate results of the present encoun-ter with crisis are characteristically "postmodern": the final dismem-berment of the "individual" represented by the assembled faculties of the institution, and the simultaneous evacuation of the university as a space for meaningful work or knowable history.

Paradoxically, people who depend on the liberal arts for em-ployment are consequently in a better position than anyone else to understand what is happening to the society at large, since as a class they have already been subjected, however willingly, to the forces transforming it. Their peripheral status has placed them fortuitously, if also prophetically, at the center of things. At the same time, because exposure has made them vulnerable, they are perhaps not likely to indulge a truly disinterested curiosity.

Within the representational space of the university, the unre-presentative life loses all authority: it cannot originate language, or value. But given the institutionalized role of "criticism," the critic cannot avoid being unrepresentative, particularly now that the liberal arts have come to play such a minor role in the practical life of students in particular and, by extension, the "culture" in general. Arnold, it should be remembered, never imagined the critic as an institutional fixture, an academic man. For him criticism remained a public activity, though one whose value depended upon institutional representations. The professor, or don, alone was a full-time resident of the "culture," to which others might potentially refer; his virtue depended upon the unproductive purity of his "liberal" pursuits, as Cardinal Newman conceived of them: "That alone is liberal knowl-edge which stands on its own pretensions, which is independent of sequel, expects no complement, refuses to be *informed* (as it is called) by any end, or absorbed into any art, in order duly to present itself to our contemplation."[1] Thus Arnold's insistence on "disinterest-edness," because most practitioners of criticism had to make their way in the world, just as he did, and they had to be wary of appearing too much of it if they wanted to preserve the status of their own representations and the alliance between middle-class experience and the supposed timelessness of "liberal knowledge." "Disinterestedness," then, was merely a way of economizing a particular and *interested* version of truth: one founded on the claim to authority that the university represented, on the institution of a knowledge "which stands on its own pretensions." For the critic, particularly one so politically involved as Arnold, there were obvious rhetorical advantages to a discursive stance "which is independent of sequel, expects no complement . . . in order duly to present itself to our contemplation."

Obviously, present conditions are different, which accounts for the contradictory position of the contemporary academic who, on the one hand, represents the sequestered life of culture (a life that crisis has rendered specially prominent, and often culpable), and, on the other, must account for his time in terms of a salable, critical product: "It is assumed that all candidates for tenure will be actively engaged in and professionally committed to scholarly research and publication of the results of that research since these activities are the clearest indications of intellectual development. They are the principal means of enhancing this department's reputation on national and international levels."[2] The above quotation comes from a departmental tenure document, one written by senior faculty to explain the narrative of academic growth to their junior colleagues.

Central to this explanation, obviously, is a traditional model of production. Work(s) become a representation of the individual for whom they stand, just as the individual represents (through work) the "reputation" of the institution, the value of the one defining the characterological worth of the other: "While not wishing to discourage diversity of interests, the department encourages a candidate to develop an area of expertise. In establishing the quality of published and accepted work, the department will consider its nature and scope as well as the selectivity and reputation of the journals and presses that publish the material" (pp. 4–5). The narrative economy instituted here—one based on production, improvement, "coherent" growth of character, market value, and surveillance—has been fundamental to industrial societies and their representative institutions for the last hundred and fifty years. In that sense the document is not special in its demands. On the contrary, the emphasis on "research" as a representation of character is typical, and typically acceptable—at least statistically—among academics, 55 percent of whom agree that it is very hard to get tenure without publishing, but less than 17 percent of whom (including faculty at liberal arts colleges) feel that their field is too research-oriented.[3]

"Good work," likewise, is what the university represents—virtually—to the majority of Americans. According to a recent Gallup poll (May 1985), the public's belief in the importance of education has grown every year since 1978; currently 90 percent of parents with public-school children say that they would like their oldest child to attend college. As to what college represents, the figures are equally clear. When asked what they felt to be the advantages of a college education (if any), the highest percentage (52 percent) answered job opportunities, or getting a better job. The next most frequent response (18 percent) was that college proved useful because it led to a higher income. At the bottom of the list of reasons for attending college were the Newman/Arnold ideals of maturation (6 percent) and a belief that college teaches a person to think (3 percent), both of which finished lower than the responses of no advantage/other/don't know (combined 8 percent).[4] Whether the findings of this poll represent the truth about college, or whether they ought to, isn't the point. The point is that for the great majority of Americans, most of whom will never go there, college has a representational function that is tied specifically to work. Colleges are worth supporting, and worth attending, because the people in them know what it means to work and can help other people get ahead.

This public attitude is reflected in the attitude of officials, such as state governors, who concluded, succinctly, in a recent report of their national association, that "better schools mean better jobs."[5] Along with this expectation goes the corollary that if one wants better jobs, the schools must be held accountable, their work must be submitted to quality control, which is a demand that the governors share with the secretary of education: "The Department of Education has an obligation to the students it assists with financial aid and to the taxpayers whose funds it disburses to suggest better means by which the higher education consumer can be confident he is purchasing a sound product."[6] As is evidenced by the departmental tenure handbook cited above, this same expectation informs the thinking of academics themselves: "Tenure decisions obviously play a vital role in shaping the long-term quality of the department. Hence the most important factor in tenure deliberations must be our common desire to foster excellence" (p. 1). By common agreement, then, good work is what the university is all about. But the agreement is only apparent—a trick of language—for which language and the people responsible for it are likely to suffer.

Given the convergent economy of expectation that sustains the modern university as a meaningful representation, the results for those who "work" there are immediate, particularly for those in the humanities, whose only "product" is language, and who originate—presumptively if not actually—the language by means of which the university accounts for itself as a whole: "Through its teaching, the University undertakes to provide each student, at undergraduate and graduate levels, with experiences leading to a broadening of intellectual horizons, to a satisfying, meaningful life and to continuing intellectual growth exemplifying a truly liberal education."[7] Thus the bland familiarity, and reassurance, of catalog discourse. Nothing could sound more traditional, even though the institution—especially its literature department, where Greek and Latin are never taught and almost never read—would probably prove unrecognizable to Matthew Arnold and John Henry Newman.

As a matter of fact, my school, whose catalog I just quoted from, would more likely appeal to Thomas Huxley, Arnold's opponent in the great Victorian debates over education, who was bitterly critical of a "liberal education" and the ignorance he felt it imposed as regards the contemporary life of a society: "I believe there can be no doubt that the foreigner who should wish to become acquainted with the scientific, or the literary, activity of modern England, would simply lose his time and his pains if he visited our universities with that object."[8] The school where I work is a large urban university, part of the state system; it was built on behalf of the very practical needs that Huxley argued for. But regardless of the nature of visible, institutional signifiers—curricular course requirements, and so on—and the role that work has come to play in academic careers, the incantatory power of Arnold's "liberal" formulations is such that the great signified of "culture" remains at the very center of our notion of what we do and why we do it (whether for or against), with obvious consequences both for language and the people who make it.

Language, in itself, has come to the center of things because culture no longer can. It's not that *medium* has emerged as *message*; it's more that the message has become irrelevant, so that the medium is all there is left; and it, at least, is tangible, quantifiable with reference to work, whether of the real or the service variety. Culture, then, has necessarily been reinterpreted as a displaced form of work. Critical language, like the institution it sustains, is representational: it represents work whose value is realized only outside the place of production, just like a Chevrolet can't yield a profit until it leaves the factory and becomes a commodity. Once again, the departmental tenure handbook: "Tenure candidates should recognize that refereed scholarly publication remains the single most important criterion for tenure in the Department . . . and in the deliberations of college and university committees" (p. 5). The academic "community" becomes a surrogate for the now dissipated culture; they, or their standards, "referee" the valuation of individual careers. This is true of all critical productions, regardless of their meta-stance as regards representation. *Culture, absence, history,* for example, are all representations the value of which is not intrinsic but dependent on market conditions. Texts that once yielded *irony* and *tension* now yield *différance* or *power,* which is only to be expected because the one sells and the other doesn't.

As far as the actual inmates of the institution are concerned, such changes are of little or no concern, since critical language is not intended for them in the first place: students can't understand it; and service employees have no need of it, since their careers are based on alternative forms of production. And the approval of one's professorial colleagues—though gratifying—counts for relatively little compared with prominent publication. Academic careers are scripted for a virtual community, then, rather than a real one, which makes the modern "critical" role a much different affair than it was for Arnold, or Mill, say. Even when the academic enters society as an "expert," her/his values consists in difference, in the possession of special knowledge, rather than common interest. As to the comforts of virtual community, that may be why more than a third of all academics say they are considering another career, with the highest rate of discontent coming among the faculty of liberal arts colleges of medium size, where 43 percent feel they may leave the profession within the next five years. These are the places that Newman and Arnold had in mind when they wrote about the "idea" of a university, about the life of the "best self." Whatever has gone wrong with those lofty representations has gone most conspicuously wrong at the very place where the consolations of liberal knowledge, and practice, ought to be the most keenly felt.[9]

In order to understand what may, or may not, have happened, it is necessary to consider what has become of language in the modern university, and how the present differs from the past. A professor's work in Arnold's time consisted more of talking, reading aloud, and perhaps even doing some creative writing. The professor came by his credentials because he spent his life producing and reproducing the text of culture. There is, for example, the following letter (3 December 1882) by the American novelist William Dean Howells, which proposes a program of instruction at Johns Hopkins University:

> I do feel strongly and deeply, the art of literature, and I believe I could make others feel its beauty and importance. . . . When I had acquainted myself fully with the literary attainments and opinions of the class and come perfectly into *rapport* with them, I should want to see their work, to criticize it with them and correct it—not in detail but "by sample." All the time I should be giving illustrative readings and lectures, which would be rather to the point of what we were doing than in any order of time, or critical or historical sequence. Often I should read a poem, or an essay or passage from a novel or history, and prove to them— for such things are perfectly susceptible of proof—why it was good or bad; but I should always give them the first chance to analyze: I should seek at every step to make them partners in the enterprise, and not treat them as bottles to be filled with so much literary information and opinion.[10]

The plan was acceptable, apparently, but Howells declined the professorship of literature that was offered him: the salary was too little; he could make more money writing novels full time.

But both the proposal and the reasons for declining are indicative. On the one hand, Howells's prospectus was accepted as a representation of what a professor of liberal arts, specifically literature, ought to be doing; on the other, he chose to refuse because an academic "living" would not support his style of life, although neither he nor those who proposed and supported his appointment saw any essential difference between the "work" of a professor and that of a novelist. On the contrary, the one constituted Howells's qualification for the other. As to formal education, he had quit school at fourteen; but his success as an editor and fiction writer entitled him to assume the duties of teacher. The activities of both careers were representative of culture, wages in the one instance simply being better than those in the other.

This contrasts markedly with the position of a contemporary academic and the texts he or she has charge of. Today there is a marketplace too, as I have suggested, but the work for which one is rewarded (writing) is different from, even antithetical to, both the work that, day by day, one is expected to do (teaching) and the "works" on which one practices, with the professor no longer engaged in creating language of the same order as that being professed. Novelists write novels, and poets write poems; but literature teachers write something else—something not usually understood by their constituents. This difference makes for a significant change in the status of the texts comprising the canon of professional practice. For Howells or for Arnold, say, a literary work was valuable because it represented life at its purest and most heightened state of culture. As Arnold wrote in responding to Thomas Huxley, "If there is to be separation and option between humane letters on the one hand, and the natural sciences on the other, the great majority of mankind . . . would do well . . . to be educated in humane letters. . . . Letters will call out their being at more points, will make them live more."[11] Literature, in other words, was about living—living the exemplary life of culture, which was the virtual destination of all those for whom the academy represented an answer to the question of self-production. The job of the critic/teacher was pedagogical in the strictest sense of that word: the job of one who leads another toward a desired destination, whether from inside or outside the academy. The distinction of outside/inside was largely irrelevant, however, as Howells's case shows, because novelist, or critic, and professor were engaged with producing the same large text, the text of culture.

This idea still—or again—has considerable force, particularly in the wake of the various "isms" that overtook literary study in the 1960s and 1970s. For example, Roger Shattuck published an influential article several years ago in which he incarnates a figure very much like Howells: an aging professor who simply reads to his class instead of preaching theory at them. Over time, Shattuck says, he has come to appreciate the value of what the old professor is doing.[12] People like the contributors to the *Critical Inquiry* special issue that urges a separation of teaching and theory might be expected to respond sympathetically to this notion of professorial practice. To me, though, Shattuck's article seems pretty unrealistic: his ideas don't represent the economy of work that determines the lives of academics, especially those who haven't yet achieved tenure and a chair to sit it out in. Also, I wonder how many of the students in the old professor's audience—students who've come to school expecting to get some *work* done—would respect a teacher who apparently had nothing to say, whether they understood it or not.

However romantically appealing, Shattuck's model doesn't represent meaningful work. But work is what academics get paid and promoted for doing, and it is only on the basis of work, visibly produced and valued, that the academy can continue in its representational function. Furthermore, insofar as teaching is supposed to represent the sharing of one's work—as Howells and Arnold, for example, imagined that it ought to do—literature in the modern university ceases being about life and begins being about criticism instead. By this I don't mean the teaching of theory as such, which is the parodic antithesis that Shattuck imagines for his benign professor. Rather, I mean the use of theory to see through the now arbitrary text of culture to what is "real" in the lives of those who profess it, and—however willingly—are subjected to it. It is in this sense that the professor comes by the universalizing assumptions such as characterize the work of deconstructionists, say, or Marxists. They have understood the illusion that holds everyone else in thrall; they have made language give up its dark secrets. The only problem is that they are probably the only ones still held in thrall in the first place. For the majority of students, the falsity and irrelevance of literary culture are givens, so that critical endeavors simply replace one text with another equally mendacious one. The problem, in other words, is not with this or that version of literature but with the authority, the believability, of institutional representations generally.

By contrast, in the "classic" university, writer and critic were on the same side, like Arnold and Howells, and on the same side as their students, for whom the language of culture provided a viable class idiom. (Arnold did, in fact, become a professor at the last.) Their project can be judged either good or ill, depending upon one's point of view. But unquestionably the status of language was different because all parties to the academic undertaking were capable of contributing to the same text, although that was soon to change. As Michael Warner has pointed out in his study of literature departments, the "genteel" tradition, of which Howells and Arnold are representative, was displaced by an emerging professional class, whose careers were independent of "culture." Instead, the new professors relied on scholarly, or scientific, credentials to constitute their profession—specifically, philological study modeled on that of the German universities. And by the turn of the century, they had come to dominate the academic marketplace, the Modern Language Association, which they founded, being their primary vehicle. With this domination came the now familiar institution of professional "criticism," and its dissolution of the common idiom that characterized the assumptions of someone such as Howells. "Professional critics," Warner points out, "were thus forced to be anti-literary, in the culture's terms, in order to control the literary in institutions."[13] From that point forward, teachers and students could no longer do the same things because they no longer had access to a common language—at least, not inside the institution.

The present situation merely represents a further "scientification" of critical practice, abetted by the increasingly technical mission of the university. The assumption now, under the economy of work, is that there is written inside the texts of culture the virtual script of value, just as ingots of unforged steel could be said to contain a virtual Chevrolet. The work of an academic consists in discovering that script, and then seeing it into profitable production. Modern "criticism" is different, then, from its nineteenth-century origins, at which point writer, critic, and even student might all work toward the same end: the accumulation of the best that had been thought and said in the world, as Arnold put it. The language of culture—which one might meaningfully exchange as a token of identity—was merely an expression of a common enterprise. Therefore, it made perfect sense for Howells to think of his proposed course in literature as a course of writing: "When I had acquainted myself fully with the literary attainments and opinions of the class and come perfectly into *rapport* with them, I should want to see their work, to criticize it with them and correct it. . . . In every way I would try to emancipate them from the sense of drudgery, and yet teach them that work—delightful work—was perpetually necessary in literary art as in every other." (*Letters*, 3:45) This program made sense because everyone in it had come to the university on behalf of the same language; the university defined a space where their several projects converged, and where the culture was most visibly represented. Whether or not things ever really worked this way, or whether they ought to, is not the point; that great numbers of people spoke and wrote as if it were possible for language to accomplish such ends is what mattered.

As I said, the primary difference between then and now—between *culture* and *work*—is that teachers and students are no longer working on the same thing, even though everyone expects the academy to provide a practical apprenticeship for its clients. Unlike the writing of culture, modern criticism is not concurrent with its object—absence, history, power, and so on. It can merely refer to these things by scripting the former texts of culture for a representative (and usually self-incriminating) performance. That performative text, then, becomes the object of critical production: books, articles, monographs, conference papers, reviews, and such. However, the value of these productions cannot be realized until they leave the academic space and enter the larger scholarly marketplace/community. Here, under the dispensation of post-theory, the texts of culture become secondary to the critical script; they are made to seem less for having yielded to the critic's desire. Reversing the familiar terms of Barthes, one might say that, in the nineteenth century, professors helped *write* the text of culture, and now they are *reading* it, except that the thing they are reading about is not culture, which has lost its representational value, but criticism, which has supplanted culture, because it *works*.

And as everybody—or almost everybody—agrees, from Roger Shattuck to a panel of experts who were queried by the editors of *New Literary History*, criticism, in its professional/theoretical aspect, is something that students—especially undergraduate students—ought to be spared. Raymond Federman, of the State University of New York at Buffalo, summed up the matter nicely. "In other words," he said, "too often literary theory abandons literature."[14] That is precisely the point, and also the problem. Students are being summoned back in ever greater numbers, given the present "crisis," to study something—literature—that their teachers have long since seen through, thanks to the theoretical preoccupations that have become a necessary part of our professional marketplace. But what the teachers saw when they got through literature—which is criticism—is something that students—at least the majority of them—are never going to get a look at.

This is not to say that a person may not still believe in literature in the old way, and in fact many students—at least the ones who are still in the habit of reading—seem to do just that. They speak unselfconsciously about what poems and novels "mean" and about what their authors "intended." Teachers, of course, have the option of adopting these same ideas, although they must be more circumspect. Imagine, for instance, the consequences if someone now were to make a statement such as this at a professional meeting: "More and more mankind will discover that we have to turn to poetry to interpret life for us, to console us, to sustain us. Without poetry, our science will appear incomplete; and most of what now passes with us for religion and philosophy will be replaced by poetry" (Arnold, p. 306). The quotation is from Matthew Arnold's "The Study of Poetry." As a poet, he might be excused his naïveté, even now perhaps; as a critic he probably would not be. In either case he was wrong, statistically if not existentially, as the enrollment figures of any English department will show: more and more we have come to discover that poetry courses don't register. But then he was writing a long time ago.

Or perhaps it would be more accurate to think of this distance as spatial rather than temporal because, in the long history of universities, Arnold is not chronologically far off at all, as his vernacular availability makes clear, although the space he inhabited was vastly different from mine. However anachronistic, my students and I still assemble at the same old place, the university, and we are called here by the same discursive program. But we no longer share the same space, insofar as space is defined by a meaningful economy of production. They have their agenda, and I have mine; and these are not the same, which is apparently just how they will remain. For the student, "getting over" required courses is a primary goal—like getting over mono. The quicker it's behind you, the better, because then you can get on to the subjects that really matter—i.e., those that refer to real-world work experiences. And given the elective unprofitability of the liberal arts, they are rarely encountered in any other than a required context. For the professor the reward structure of academic life implies the same vacuity as regards pedagogy. Junior professors, who are unproved, have to teach more courses, and certainly more undergraduate requirements, than their senior colleagues, whose worth is credited by their being "freed" from teaching in order to get their *own* work done. And if a professor becomes truly successful, on a national or international level, she/he is relieved from teaching altogether. For the service employees who take up the slack, there is surely nothing real about academic space, where they are permanent aliens: neither students nor professionals. Within the classroom, then, nobody is at home, and the (once) common language of culture is what makes everyone strangers. It is the lie under whose cover a whole range of mutually frustrating activities goes forward.

Except for the burden of bad faith, however, there might be no penalty to pay, so long as the lie went unattended: a purely "academic" matter. But given the current prominence, and politicization, of the academy, attention has been focused on it with a rare intensity, and for precisely the reasons that the discourse of culture would invite. Speaking at the ceremonies marking the three hundred fiftieth anniversary of Harvard University, Secretary Bennett, for example, described that university as "a representative institution of American higher education," and then went on to offer the following criticism: "There is an extraordinary gap between the rhetoric and the reality of American higher education. The gap is so wide, in fact, that we face the real possibility—not today, perhaps not tomorrow, but someday—of an erosion of public support for the enterprise."[15] The university will be made to pay, in other words, for trivializing language, for lying. And this is a problem special to the liberal arts and the supposed reinstitution of a "core curriculum," which has been a typical—and typically profitable—response to crisis. "I think students would benefit from a real core curriculum," Mr. Bennett said, "*i.e.*, a *set* of fundamental courses, ordered, purposive, coherent. I cannot discern such a core curriculum here'' (p. 28). Nor is he likely to, and for the precise reasons he suggests.

Academic careers are formulated, as Michael Warner points out, on a scientific basis, which makes essential the professionalization and the departmentalization of knowledge. That is the historical source of present institutional formations, which displaced the genteel ''culture'' of William Dean Howells and Matthew Arnold. The problem now is that the university never developed a discourse to go along with its emerging professional structure, so that the more ''modern'' the institution became, the bigger the lie it represented in terms of its ostensible ''liberal'' nature. And now William Bennett arrives, spokesman for a pervasive new literalism—a belief that representations, whether academic or otherwise, must be taken seriously:

> Under the heading of the Core Curriculum we find an agglomeration of courses, many of them obviously meaty and important, taught by eminent scholars, on a wide variety of subjects. But it seems to me that many of them could more appropriately find their place among the individual offerings of the various departments of instruction, from where, indeed, they give every appearance of having been plucked, only to be regrouped in new combinations. (P. 28)

Thus the lie of liberal discourse, the ''extraordinary gap between the rhetoric and the reality of American higher education.'' And insofar as the institution remains representational, there can be no end to lying because there is nobody in it to speak for culture, for a ''core'' experience, except as imaginary or historical formulations. That is not the job of academics, nor has it been for a great many years, regardless of what they may have said.

In the absence of a common script of value, then, the activity going on inside the institution and the language that it produces are no more exigent than the air that inflates a swimming pool canopy in January. This language, like the air, has meaning only while it remains trapped, and it is produced only for that reason. Once released, it disappears, which means that the work required to produce it is rendered irrelevant as regards the representation of value in the ''real'' world. Old term papers, like old lecture notes, for example, have meaning only within the institution; we can't expect anybody outside a classroom to show an interest in such things, including ourselves once we leave here. Both my students and I want to get on with our lives, then, and with the work necessary to support them; but the space we inhabit—or the requirements that constitute the space—prevent us. As a result, the language that defines our relations and renders them quantifiable (and demonstrable) as work—the language of lectures, notes, papers, exams, reports, presentations, evaluations, and grades—takes on a debilitating "lightness," to borrow Milan Kundera's term.[16] This is only made worse by the inflationary intervention of crisis. Now, in order to "buy" the same bachelor's degree, students are required to spend more time producing the anachronistic currency of the liberal arts. Similarly, professors, in order to keep their jobs, must write more articles in order to secure the same result—tenure and promotion, which, like the overproduced B.A., represents a consistently less valuable commodity.[17] Whatever goes on in class, then, is the antithesis of potential value, rather than its virtual expression.

Whether such unprofitable work will continue, or whether—as Secretary Bennett suggests—professors will be submitted to working-class supervision, along with their writing-class colleagues, remains to be seen. In either case, though, it is language that suffers. Like the wheelbarrow full of Second Reich marks, its reference grows so nebulous as to become more a curiosity than an article of belief— a souvenir of meaning rather than its actuality—thus the paradox of academic production, and its inevitable tendency toward "lightness":

> The heaviest of burdens is therefore simultaneously an image of life's most intense fulfillment. The heavier the burden, the closer our lives come to the earth, the more real and truthful they become. Conversely, the absolute absence of a burden causes man to be lighter than air, to soar into the heights, take leave of the earth and his earthly being, and become only half real, his movements as free as they are insignificant. What then shall we choose? Weight or lightness?[18]

Because of the role that the university plays as the entry to work, and because of the crisis-generated resurgence of the liberal arts within the university, students have no choice but to elect lightness, and the freedom of inconsequence that "culture" holds out to them. And even for those who do not go far in the liberal arts, or get beyond basic comp, this is still the sign under which their activities are conducted because culture continues to write the agenda of the university in general, regardless of how emptied of significance this writing, and the experience to which it refers, may have become.

And as I said, it is language that suffers, with results achieving self-consciousness at the level of style. When words could still be relied on to put you in touch with the world, or at least with experience, style remained a sort of non-question: "Say what you have to say, what you have a will to say, in the simplest, the most direct and exact manner possible."[19] That may sound like Strunk and White, but the advice is in fact Walter Pater's, in his famous essay "Style" (1888). Pater's "modernist" situation forced upon him a new awareness of the impermanence and unreliability of the external world. But as yet, language itself remained immune to doubt—at least when it was "simple" and "direct." Or perhaps it would be more accurate to say that there was as yet no doubt about the potential truth of *representation*: "to achieve style, begin by affecting none—that is, place yourself in the background. A careful and honest writer does not need to worry about style. As he becomes proficient in the use of the language, his style will emerge, because he himself will emerge."[20] Thus the classic advice from *The Elements of Style*, which, following Pater, makes the self the guarantee of representational truth. But it is precisely the self that becomes a problem—or a problematic—in a postmodern domain, so that authenticity can no longer be assumed automatically.

In fact, the serviceable self of an inflationary postculture is multiple—or at least multiply sited—as opposed to unitary. In that sense university representations don't lie; they *do* stand for the compartmentalized and frequently overlapping competencies that constitute a successful—if not necessarily coherent—individual life. And within that domain, new means must be found to guarantee language, since authenticity is no longer a simple matter of references. "This is, no doubt, the moment to say something about style," Fredric Jameson proposes, for example, in the introduction to his study *Marxism and Form*.[21] And what he sets out to do is defend a kind of language that modernist critics or writers might refer to, disparagingly, as "opaque." But it is precisely opacity of surface that now stands for, that takes the place of, a shared belief in, and the consequent authority of, reference:

> Nowhere is the hostility of the Anglo-American tradition toward the dialectical more apparent, however, than in the widespread notion that the style of these works is obscure and cumbersome, indigestible, abstract—or, to sum it all up in a convenient catchword, *Germanic*. . . . What if, in this period of the overproduction of printed matter and the proliferation of methods of quick reading, they [ideals of clarity and simplicity of language] were intended to speed the reader across a sentence in such a way that he can salute a readymade idea effortlessly in passing, without suspecting that real thought demands a descent into the materiality of language and a consent to time itself in the form of the sentence? (P. xiii)

Thus the times demand a calling into question of language, or language surface. Or as Jacques Derrida has more succinctly stated this problematic, he writes so as to be untranslatable; otherwise, people would forget that he is *writing* in language.

In one way or another, people—especially disillusioned minions of culture—now seem intent upon getting even with language, their vengefulness having to do with the failure of representation, and by extension the institutions charged with representational responsibilities. Perhaps the final development in the consequent (de)volution of style comes in the writing of Bret Easton Ellis, whose *Less Than Zero* is frequently compared to *The Catcher in the Rye*, and has become a "campus classic." Ellis was a student at Bennington College when he wrote the novel. In an article for *Rolling Stone*, he explained what had gone wrong with Bennington, and one assumes, with the culture it once represented. Looking back on his first days at college, he recalls, "The people I knew who came to Bennington came primarily to be artists, and if they came not knowing exactly what they wanted to do, if they came with only a vague longing, then they figured they would sample what was going on in each of the school's divisions and then decide. . . . Overall, most stayed and continued with what a lot of their parents moaned about with worry, apprehension and dread—their 'liberal-arts education.' "[22] What he laments, in words that echo Arnold and Newman, is the *interested* view of subsequent classes, which he imagines to contain increasing numbers of lawyers, engineers, doctors, and Republicans—all those who would dispel his own cherished vision: "A vision undistorted by the pressures of commerce" (p. 78). He's nostalgic for the "idea" of the university.

My concern, though, is not for his longing but for the paradigmatic form it takes, as language. Having been deceived by the economy of institutional representation, Ellis turns upon language; or he uses language to turn upon and diminish the *idea* of representation, the result being his best-selling novel, *Less Than Zero*:

> Before I left, a woman had her throat slit and was thrown from a moving car in Venice; a series of fires raged out of control in Chatsworth, the work of an arsonist; a man in Encino killed his wife and two children. Four teenagers, none of whom I knew, died in a car accident on Pacific Coast Highway. Muriel was readmitted to Cedars-Sinai. A guy, nicknamed Conan, killed himself at a fraternity party at U.C.L.A. And I met Alana accidentally in The Beverly Center.[23]

His proliferating uninflections and discontinuities become as inflationary as the general economy, whose crisis they represent and are dependent upon. This is not Hemingway's distrust of words; there's something more to it. The whole *situation* of language is becoming different. Ellis seems to be taking revenge against the *representability* of anything; and language is the medium he uses. Anything subject to representation—his *attitude* toward representation—is here subject to consequent disauthentication, including—perhaps most of all—the "self" that is a nominal source of language. It might be possible to write his work off, along with his sales, as mere adolescent posturing. But perhaps there's more to it than that, given the specific postcultural setting that he invokes. Perhaps he has dramatized the experience of "culture" represented by the university: an experience that turns him back upon the agent of his own exploitation.

5. Teachers and Students

The problem for both teachers and students is that once culture loses its ideological function, it ceases to be good for much of anything and becomes instead a matter of patently arbitrary language, an exhausted fetish. To think of Arnold's project (and the universities built to institutionalize it) as un-ideological, then, is a fundamental mistake. For reasons of emotional safety, not to mention political expediency, it may be desirable to pretend innocence, and to project it backward onto the nineteenth century. But this does little to change the facts, or to make the contemporary situation understandable. On the contrary, so long as the university remains ignorant ideologically, there will be no alternative to the bankrupt discourse of culture, which merely reveals a collective failure at self-consciousness, along with the present triviality of the liberal arts. Arnold's "disinterested" agenda succeeded because it dealt effectively with the crisis that transformed ecclesiastical institutions into modern, democratic ones. The "idea" represented by the university was one with an *interested* genealogy, which is what I mean by *ideology*. The present crisis is different; work has supplanted culture as the problem that the university must solve. And in that context, the comforts of nostalgia have already shown themselves to be cold indeed.

Arnold, by contrast, was a pragmatist; he thought of culture as representing the best self, and the best self as the foundation of a modern bureaucratic state. That is a political position, the basis of the great "compromise" by means of which the middle class entered

93

the service of Victorian society. And if the empire can be taken as evidence, it was a very effective compromise indeed. Arnold's "disinterestedness" is likewise a political, an ideological, position, through which he appropriated to the experience of a single class, his own, the virtue of universality. It was their experience of arrival that the university institutionalized. After all, it was not the upper class who needed "reform"; it was only people who stood to gain who would profit by changing the way things were.

By the acquisition of culture, and the disinterested judgment made possible through an acquaintance with the "best that had been thought and said in the world," Arnold qualified himself, and those like him, to pronounce critically on a whole range of contemporary— and frequently political—issues, the debate with Huxley over university curricula being a notable case in point. In fact, *Culture and Anarchy*, which now gets quoted in support of a non-ideological position by such authorities as Secretary Bennett, was a political pamphlet written in response to the tearing down of the Hyde Park railings during a demonstration on behalf of parliamentary reform, Arnold's position being that society needed no further reforming, now that the middle class were in charge.

In a more general sense, it was the culture represented by the university that became the basis for Victorian "Liberalism," as George Eliot has her imaginary "radical" Felix Holt explain to a mob of inflamed workingmen, a mob much like the one that did the mischief in Hyde Park and provoked Arnold to write *Culture and Anarchy*:

> There are many things—many precious benefits—which we, by the very fact of our privations, our lack of leisure and instruction, are not so likely to be aware of and take into our account. Those precious benefits form a chief part of what I may call the common estate of society. . . . I mean that treasure of knowledge, science, poetry, refinement of thought, feeling, and manners, great memories and the interpretation of great records, which is carried on from the minds of one generation to the minds of another. . . . It can make a man's life very great, very full of delight . . . it also yields a great deal of discovery that corrects error, and of invention that lessens bodily pain, and must at last make life easier for all.[1]

The implied agenda here is clear enough; it is the meliorist narrative of hard work and upward mobility, which displaced the radicalism that the Victorian bourgeoisie had come justifiably to fear.

And the reason for such effective displacement is that the "great memories" of culture could in fact be exchanged—in society—so as to "buy" gentility when personal history had failed to provide it. (It is this same agenda that led my own father—who was a working-man—to send me to a university, where I remain to this day, along with many colleagues whose hired cultural credentials are similar to mine.) Very few workingmen or radicals read Felix Holt's speech, however, since it was printed in *Blackwood's*, the readership of which were gentlemen, a great number of whom owed their position in the world to the ideological utility of the culture they acquired "at university," and which they were doubtless pleased to see credited by a "representative" of the lower orders. The time for the Felixes of the world was as yet thirty years and a war away, though they too would arrive under the same sponsorship, discursively, that George Eliot imagined. Paul Morel, for instance, was no less a man of "culture" than his Victorian forebears, though Lawrence never felt easy about having traded history in for an imaginary past. And like a great many others, both before and after, he began looking for an external agent to blame for his disfranchisement, when the responsible party, ideologically, lay much closer to home.

That is only to be expected. Almost from the beginning of the modern university's history, people have been trying to deprive it— or its "culture"—of ideological implications, making of it instead a self-referential icon, the exposed arbitrariness of which yields the present crisis of confidence:

> At the very moment when the scope of literary culture has increasingly contracted to the university, the educational function of literature has become increasingly amorphous. The loss of belief—or loss of interest—in literature as a means of understanding weakens the educational claims of literature and leaves the literature teacher without a rationale for what he professes. Students are quick to perceive that their teachers no longer hold the naïve view that literature can explain anything.[2]

The charge, made by Gerald Graff in *Literature against Itself* (1979), is familiar enough by now, and surely often enough repeated. Yet the belief persists that literature in particular and the humanities in general have somehow been, and should remain, ideologically pure— a belief that leads to the banalizing self-defeat that Graff describes.

William Bennett, for example, can demand purity while at the same time proposing a core curriculum based on such works as Machiavelli, Wordsworth, Dickens, Marx, Martin Luther King, and the Declaration of Independence. It is impossible to imagine how one might remain non-ideological—either in print or in the classroom— while living up to the secretary's announced standard of excellence for teachers, his insistence that "they are moved and are seen to be moved by the power of the works [they present] and are able to convey that power to their students."[3] To reduce King's "Letter from the Birmingham Jail," for instance, to a matter of rhetorical appreciation—however intense—is both ridiculous and insulting. However, Mr. Bennett is not unique in his dread of ideology—merely typical. Arnold too proposed a critical "disinterest," so that he might speak the desire of his own class as if it were the revealed voice of nature. And he was probably honest in his belief that a middle-class culture, such as he imagined, would define a millennial ideal, the social vanishing point of "progress." That he was wrong is no scandal; that we should repeat his error is.

In this context literary modernism can be taken as indicative both of the arbitrariness of "culture" and of its consequent vulnerability. And if one accepts Yeats's designation of Walter Pater as the first modernist writer, his case becomes paradigmatic, since he came earlier to the disillusionments that motivate such characteristic—and characteristically middle-class—movements as postmodernism and de-construction.

Pater's arrival at Brasenose College, Oxford, is typical of a more general arrival, which the university made possible: the arrival of the middle class in society. Educational institutions now extended the franchise of culture just as political institutions extended the vote. That is what it means to live in a representative democracy. Culture became a stand-in for history, and the basis on which the middle class plotted its position in the world, as William Dean Howells discovered in the genteel drawing rooms of Boston, and subsequently in the salons of literary New York. People defined themselves by reference to school, and to the ennobling experience that school represented, as was the case with Howells, whose culture came by virtue of identification rather than actual attendance. On this basis, middle-class figures like himself, or Pater, found a place, referentially, "in society." But Howells turned Hopkins down; Pater, on the other hand, undertook a career as an academic, and as a result, encountered both difficulty and insight inherent in his position, which is very like that of contemporary professors, the majority of whom came by their careers, and their places in the culture, as a result of the middle-class boom that followed World War II.

Through the agency of culture, then, Walter Pater, who was the second son of a Roman Catholic doctor, could translate himself into the Anglicized figure—and the permanent living—of an Oxford don; just as Howells, who had left school at fourteen, could have become a professor of literature, if he had chosen to do so, though in his case, a university appointment would merely have confirmed a distinction already established in the popular understanding. Pater, on the other hand, would not have become "somebody" except for his job. And that's where things began to go wrong.

Pater's problem—and the origin of his "modernist" discovery—was that he had come to *represent* culture, as opposed to Howells or Arnold, who continued, as outsiders, to appeal to, and profit by, a truth that he now embodied. Having "earned" his reward, he had been deprived of further expectations; and that deprivation turned him inward, upon the agents of his own arrival—upon the language out of which an increasingly unbelievable signified was composed:

> If we continue to dwell in thought on this world, not of objects in the solidity with which language invests them, but of impressions, unstable, flickering, inconsistent, which turn and are extinguished with our consciousness of them, it [the inner, like the outer, life] contracts still further: the whole scope of observation is dwarfed to the narrow chamber of the individual mind. . . . To such a tremulous wisp constantly reforming itself on the stream, to a single sharp impression, with a sense in it, a relic more or less fleeting of such moments gone by, what is real in our life fines itself down. It is with this movement, with the passage and dissolution of impressions, images, sensations, that analysis leaves off—that continual vanishing away, that strange, perpetual weaving and unweaving of ourselves.[4]

In place of some inherently satisfying "truth," Pater finds merely "impressions, images, sensations," with which "analysis leaves off." If there were anything *real* to be grasped, he—by definition—would know it, given his situation. He *is* the individual whom culture has made. But what he knows, and all he knows, are the momentary effects of language. And that knowledge transforms Pater into the now familiar *subject* of modernist isolation—the solitary self whose identity consists in registering (however intensely) the dissolution of all that lies outside.

Pater's situation allowed him premonitory access to a particular experience of culture. The economic collapse of "progress" and the political demise of "liberalism," along with two world wars, would eventually disperse, and literalize, this same experience throughout the middle class, who had worked hard to support an institution that afforded them little protection, either practical or intellectual, against the disasters that history had in store. For that matter, Bennett's attack on ideology, with its obvious reminder of (if not nostalgia for)

the 1950s is merely a reflex of Pater's disillusionment: the acknowl-
edgment, whether willing or grudged, that middle-class culture is a
made-up idea, the frailty of which must not be revealed. In this
connection the compensatory "inspiration" that the National Endowment for the Humanities urges on teachers and writers might
have come straight from Pater: "To burn always with this hard,
gemlike flame, to maintain this ecstasy, is success in life" (p. 158).
Whatever form this advice takes, the economy of momentary intens-
ities is inevitable to a denial of ideological purpose. And like the
consumptive's glow, it is the expression of energy with no productive
outlet.

More recently, Pater's "discovery" has been advanced by various adherents of textualism, or deconstruction, Jacques Derrida
having offered an opportune figure, or figuration, around which academics enact a variety of nostalgic disillusionments:

> Yet if reading must not be content with doubling the text, it cannot
> legitimately transgress the text toward something other than it, toward
> a referent (a reality that is metaphysical, historical, psychobiographi-
> cal, etc.) or toward a signified outside the text whose content could
> take place, could have taken place outside of language, that is to say,
> in the sense that we give here to that word, outside of writing in general.
> . . . *There is nothing outside of the text* [there is no outside-text; *il n'y
> a pas de hors-texte*]. . . . There has never been anything but writing.
> . . . We have read, *in the text*, that the absolute present, Nature, that
> which words like "real mother" name, have always already escaped,
> have never existed; that what opens meaning and language is writing
> as the disappearance of natural presence.[5]

That this language is quite difficult is obvious. Jonathan Culler, for
instance, has made a successful and helpful career out of translating
and excerpting Derrida, among other deconstructive masters. And
because of such difficulty, or rather because of the hazy, secondhand
knowledge that often characterizes practitioners of deconstruction,
it has become possible to use the figure "Derrida" to sponsor a wide-
ranging, if unintentional, anti-intellectualism among middle-class
critics whose own experience has forced upon them Pater's initial
shock of recognition: his seeing culture for what it was, together with
his frustration at being uncertain as to whom he might blame for his
misconceptions.

It is possible to read Derrida, or rather to produce a figural, pop
version of "Derrida," and through "him" to read such passages as
the one above to the effect that there is nothing *out there* but language.
The next step—which Derrida the philosopher does not take, though

his figural clients often do—is to say that because experience arrives as a text, it therefore becomes unreal. This is to misunderstand the Derridean project in a particularly revealing way—revealing of the autobiography of a class of academics who confront in mass Pater's solitary, and premonitory, disillusionment. Because it was texts that betrayed them, they assume that anything textual is unreal, and invoke the figure of Derrida as their cynical, paternal authority: a patriarchal deconstructor of alma mater and all she represents.

This misreading has produced at least two notable results, both equally unfortunate. First is an unselfconsciously parodic aping of the master's discourse, which actively, if unintentionally, confirms the worst case diagnosis of mindless deconstruction: namely, that language and absence are synonymous. Second, as teachers, Derridean enthusiasts have anachronistically revived the classic canon and the habits of literary taste associated with it. For the first time in many years, for example, the complete works of George Eliot are back in print; and she is not the only one of the great Victorian sages undergoing a postcultural revival. Along with the primary sources have come conduct manuals, literary periodicals, and all manner of reconstructive documentation. Not that there is anything wrong with the availability of texts as such. It is the use to which the texts are often put that I find questionable. As it turns out, the avidity of textualists for the cultural villainy of *presence* leads them, in an eternal return, to the supreme sources of institutional, middle-class culture, which they now force upon their students, reconstructively, so that they will then have something triumphantly to see through. But for whom is such seeing-through undertaken? Is it really for students, whose illiteracy as regards classic, bourgeois culture renders them effectively immune to its supposed entrapments? Of course not.

The backhand reconstruction and rhetorical obfuscation often undertaken on behalf of "Derrida" in particular and "theory" in general are pure—if coded—autobiography: an obsessive return to a scene of primal disillusionments. What one encounters here is an uninterrogated displacement of frustration and anxiety—an Ellis-like urge to get even with language, particularly the language of middle-class cultural representation, because it's not clear who or what else to get even with. Such confusion is understandable, perhaps, but neither admirable, nor informed. Its reductive anti-intellectualism renders useless the precise theoretical program on whose behalf many textualists ostensibly act, so that one is led to ask, who or what has made them so upset?

Far from being upsetting, the story of middle-class, academic arrival has the outward appearance of success, at least statistically. In particular, the postwar boom in American education made possible the enfranchisement of a whole generation who have found in the academy a professional life that might otherwise have remained inaccessible. This is my story too. My grandfather was a small-scale farmer, my father sold used cars, until World War II made him an officer and a gentleman. Now, thanks to the university and to culture, his son, who couldn't make it through pre-med, has nevertheless become a professional. This experience of rapid rise I share with a great many other sons and daughters of the middle class. In America, between 1960 and 1980, the number of college students increased by 250 percent, from 3 million to 11.5 million;[6] this led to a concomitant growth in faculty, the numbers of which increased by 293 percent, from 154,000 in 1960 to 451,000 in 1979.[7] Like Pater the majority of these new professors came from middle-class backgrounds (Finkelstein, p. 38), with expectations shaped by that experience. Perhaps the most fundamental of these expectations is that work well done would add up to something—something tangible and real that could be passed on. Such has been the history of my own family; that is how I got to be where I am.

But what does the academic professional have to pass on? What does her/his arrival amount to? Those were the questions that Pater confronted when he peeled back the leaves of the cultural artichoke only to find the center empty, an *absence*. They have surely gotten no easier to answer now that the symbolic entitlements of academic work have been subjected to inflationary devaluation. Who said there was anything there/here in the first place, though? Certainly no one in a position to know, least of all the hereditary representatives of privilege and gentility. The idea of a production-based culture would have been alien to them. It's the middle-class inheritors of Arnold's university, particularly the newly enfranchised masses of the baby boom, who have accepted as an article of faith, borne out by family history, the representational imperative: the expectation that time spent (by my grandfather, my father, and me, all of us on our way up) must stand for something real. We projected that faith onto a reality that production cannot adequately comprehend. Now, having arrived at the promised reward of culture, I find myself without resources to account for my unaccustomed situation. And rather than questioning my arrival as such, I turn upon the apparent instrument of my betrayal: I turn upon language itself. At least I might be led to that, particularly in an environment where the presence of "Derrida" is felt everywhere.

By contrast, members of the leisure class appear immune to upset when exposed to nonproductive labor, to the imaginative pleasures of superfluity, on which the text (if not the usefulness) of culture depends. In Oscar Wilde's hands, for example, Pater's betrayal becomes elegant paradox in "The Decay of Lying," where he laments the intrusion of "truth" into the domain of art. Wilde seems to be saying, "Well, of course," to the gasping revelations of the *Renaissance*, just as he might have done to the auto-parodic gestures of bogus deconstruction.[8] Arrivistes have a special will to believe in the *presence* of culture (and subsequently to disbelieve); theirs is an intensity peculiar to foreigners, whose expectations have ill suited them for a life of post-narrative "work."

To his credit, Pater didn't give up on language; with it he turned himself into a brilliant, textual simulacrum for the lost signified: "Experience, already reduced to a swarm of impressions, is ringed round for each one of us by that thick wall of personality through which no real voice has ever pierced on its way to us, or from us to that which we can only conjecture to be without. Every one of those impressions is the impression of the individual in his isolation, each mind keeping as a solitary prisoner its own dream of a world" (p. 157). The high-tech impressionism of a reductive deconstruction—though it may scientify or otherwise depersonalize Pater's performative solution—remains, like he was, "prisoner" to a private agenda, though without his excuse of first arrival; and without the "style" that postmodern "writing" has reduced to so much noise. And also without Derrida's insights into the *reality* of language. As a result, even Pater's subject, and intelligence, are lost to individuals whose experience can only be addressed to disjointed, post-subjective fragments, over which they have always already relinquished control. Given the academic situation, it is tempting for even skillful practitioners to surrender to disillusionment and to forget that deconstruction, whether vulgar or profound, is not an argument against meaningful action.

But, as I've suggested, perhaps the saddest feature of such empassioned, if solitary, performances is their frequent superfluity. For instance, imagine the lack of astonishment should an undergraduate of average intelligence be confronted—against the better advice of professionals—with the Derridean program. Imagine that such a student was told that her/his professor thought of "life" as if it were a kind of book, or "text," and imagine further that the professor "explained"—in language intended to baffle a person of common intelligence—that this text was not full of "truth," but "arbitrary," and "self-referential." Far from being surprising, or otherwise disillusioning, such revelations would merely confirm what most students have understood at least for the last twenty years: that culture, and the people who work for it, are trivial if not downright silly. Which leads to the conclusion of experts, already discussed, that theory has no place in the undergraduate curriculum. But it is not theory at fault so much as the theoreticians, who expect a solution from materials that are at best problematic.

If there is to be an effective counter to the boredom and cheapness that afflict the popular imagination, and the lives shaped by it, this won't come from the mock subversion of an embittered professoriate. The inflationary pressure brought to bear on both student and faculty production is symptomatic of a general giving in. In this connection the mock-theoretical program—with its vindictive, if grandiose, aim of seeing through the last two thousand years of Western culture—is simply a projection, a globalization, of the agenda for failure that the post-boom academy has adopted under the aegis of "crisis." Overburdened (and underenrolled) institutions *want* their employees to fail in order to shrink faculty size, open tenured positions, and save the cost of raises and promotions. As for students, the economy produces too few "careers" as it is. If more students would fail—or at least fail to get out of college—enrollments would go up, and there would be room in the workplace for the "truly" qualified, among them disaffected university professors, more than half of whom, according to a Carnegie Commission survey, would seriously consider taking another academic job if one were offered.[9] The pervasive negativism of attitude is obvious. Just read the review section of any scholarly journal and see how much appreciative, constructive "criticism" you find there: just about as much as you'd find if you read the comments on a set of freshman compositions, or a set of course evaluations prepared by the students who wrote the compositions. There may be no pleasure as such in the failure of others. Still, it is preferable to failure of one's own, so that preemptive strikes often become advisable, particularly in times of shrinking resources.

Rather than acknowledging what is actually happening, however, the "profession" appears locked into a self-defeating nostalgia: a vague sense of anxiety over present conditions, combined with a wish to "reclaim" some past time when things were better. According to the Carnegie Forum on Teaching as a Profession, "Because we have defined the problem of the schools in terms of decline from earlier standards, we have unwittingly chosen to face backwards when it is essential that we face forward."[10] At the same time, the report acknowledges that ideological disengagement—however alienating individually—may be preferable from a professional and social standpoint: "The American mass-education system, designed in the early part of the century for a mass-production economy, will not succeed unless it not only raises but redefines the essential standards of excellence and strives to make quality and equality of opportunity compatible with each other" (p. 45). It remains to be seen whether our society is willing to commit the massive resources necessary to "make quality and equality of opportunity compatible with each other."

Such is the challenge confronting the educational establishment as it is called on to train people for the transformation from a production-based economy to one based on information. Of course, everyone need not make this change, which is the point of the Carnegie report. Already it appears that the upward mobility traditionally associated with the middle class has been severely curtailed—to the extent that some commentators have begun to question whether the middle class will survive at all.[11] It may well be that "we" decide to abandon—as postmodern illiterates—a progressively larger segment of the population, consigning them to the perpetual idiocy (and frequent impoverishment) of permanent "service" employment, just as English professors have already done to their colleagues in "comp." If that is the case, then the innocence of "culture" will surely afford "us" a certain dubious comfort, which is perhaps why there is such reluctance—on both the left and the right—to abandon so obviously exhausted an idea, or to implicate academic work ideologically, as if it were real; and as if it ought to involve itself, really, with the work that other people are being trained to do, "out there in the world." We can't be blamed for what we had no hand in making, after all; and *culture*, whether deconstructed or merely tolerated, confers a consoling denial of results. At worst, we are simply ignorant; at best, we can say, "We told you so."

That people live, ideologically, by stories that they have invented is no disgrace. In any case, it is inevitable. The danger to be feared is that we'll forget—either innocently or out of self-interest— that our stories are made up, and therefore subject to change as well as blame. Out of weakness, or fear, or both then, we cling to the fiction of Pater's isolated subject, as if it were not the result—like any other—of historical and ideological causes. His experience has been institutionalized, as the academy, particularly in post–World War II America, becomes a mere extension of modernism and the fixed alienation that a faith in culture represents.

If there's to be an end to culture, and the debilitating limitations it imposes, the university must begin by taking seriously its representational role. If the university represents—by virtue of its assembled faculties—a model of individual life, then the unsatisfactoriness of culture, as an instrument of either analysis or self-defense, becomes at once apparent. One has only to consider the structure, and the degree requirements, of modern universities to see that the discourse of culture is not an accurate guide to the kind of individual here represented. Or, more accurately, culture no longer describes the kind of literacy that characterizes such individuals. Nor is culture sufficiently powerful, institutionally, to bother with deconstructing. For once the lie is obvious, and commonly acknowledged. Nevertheless, academics persist in adhering to this dubious *lingua franca*, whether out of belief, cynicism, or some darker, deconstructive motive; as a result, language as such has become subject to both doubt and trivialization.

For example, the secretary of education was quoted as saying that a recent study of young Americans between the ages of 21 and 25 showed that "the United States is not awash in illiteracy."[12] Yet this same study revealed that 90 percent of those surveyed could not read a four-line poem. The secretary's comment is indicative of a generally held belief that the academic individual—and the institutions that produce him or her—ought to be held accountable not according to the literacy standards of culture but according to standards relative to successful work; and for those purposes, such acquirements as poetry reading are totally irrelevant.

People may persist in generalizing about the university in Arnold's outmoded idiom—with varying degrees of faith, both good and bad—because we lack a more accurate or acceptable one. But when it comes to evaluating the individuals produced by the academy, there is neither embarrassment nor confusion. In summarizing the findings of the National Governors' Association report, "Time for results: The Governors' 1991 Report on Education," the chairman, Governor Lamar Alexander, of Tennessee, said the following: "Better schools mean better jobs. Unless states face these questions, Americans won't keep our high standard of living. To meet stiff competition from workers in the rest of the world, we must educate ourselves and our children as we never have before."[13] The shift in emphasis from culture to work seems only reasonable, if not necessarily desirable, insofar as a society organized by information and media coverage (as opposed to the linear, text-based forms associated with high culture and the production economy it represented) demands a new literacy for those who are to function efficiently and make their way in the world.

At the same time, the discourse of culture provides a powerful opportunity, managerially, to address—and domesticate—the academy at a moment of social transformation and crisis, which is why so many public officials subscribe to an Arnoldian idiom. "Good work" has become essential—a national duty—in these days of fierce, warlike competition; and if this is to become a "nation prepared," people must be taught how to work efficiently. In this environment the academy makes itself vulnerable to judgment and blame by adopting, or merely acquiescing in, the language of culture. Academics must either stand behind culture as defense and apologia or else admit to having committed themselves to irrelevancy. But in neither instance is the issue a happy one. Either the university has been telling the truth about itself all along, in which case Newman's time-honored "idea" has finally proved unworkable, as Secretary Bennett's comments on illiteracy would lead one to believe; or else it has been lying as deconstructionists and various other apostates are happy to point out. Either way, surveillance and external management are called for, since academics are obviously incapable, at present, of managing their own affairs.

The academy is still the place—however unfortunately—that the society must turn for specialized training such as will be required if we are to industrialize information as we once did production; and since our economic survival is at stake, extraordinary measures are justified, just as they always have been in times of "war." Not surprisingly, then, the federal government has initiated moves toward a nationalized curricular control, as I have already pointed out. "The Department of Education has an obligation to the students it assists with financial aid and to the taxpayers whose funds it disburses," Secretary Bennett has been quoted as saying, "to suggest better means by which the higher education consumer can be confident he is purchasing a sound product."[14] The values implicit in such a statement would have been anathema to Arnold, for whom the university represented a symbolic alternative to marketplace thinking rather than an overt extension of mercantilism.

The secretary is being neither two-faced nor inconsistent, however, when he invokes culture on the one hand and on the other demands a federalized, consumerist surveillance. Rather, he is typical of the analysis that follows upon the non-ideological interpretation of the academy, particularly in its present, modernist—or post-modernist—orientation. The disciplinary text of culture is merely being re-economized according to an alternate interpretation of value: one based on work rather than social mobility. The literate individual, whose competence, or "faculties," the academy virtually represents, is now expected to perform in a more profitable way. What is called for, then, is not actually new so much as it is a reinterpretation of extant, disciplinary standards, which is why the discussion can reasonably be conducted (at least from a bureaucratic standpoint) using the otherwise outmoded language of culture. Precisely because our ahistorical text is unencumbered by an experiential signified, such change is—or ought to be—a simple enough matter, so that measurement—proficiency—rather than canon becomes the focus of educational debates.

In practical terms the outmoded "individual" represented by the assembled faculties of the university is being colonized by the agents of superior values, who like all colonialists proceed with the best interests of the native subject at heart—just as Arnold proceeded with his conversion of hereditary privilege to the superior faith of the "best self." Thus far such colonizing has gone forward unopposed; and for good reason, since there is no indigenous "faith" to counter it. As Hans Magnus Enzensberger has argued, regarding the anachronism of culture in an informational society: "The divergence between economic position and consciousness will continue to grow. . . . The so-called privileges of education have lost their fearfulness. . . . One's cultural caste will henceforth depend on personal choice, not origin. . . . Culture cannot, and need not any longer, serve the interests of a ruling class. It no longer legitimates the social order. In this sense, it has become useless."[15] The reason for this change is that the literate individual of culture has been displaced, both representatively and practically, by a different sort of individual possessed of a different, more clearly relevant, literacy.

If one were to examine statistics alone—particularly in view of the much-discussed transformation to an information-based society—the facts might appear contradictory. According to the federal study already cited, 75 percent of whites between the ages of 21 and 25 are partially if not completely incompetent in the category of "document literacy": "using information in documents such as charts, maps and tables." (The percentages for Hispanics and blacks are even higher, 93 and 97 percent respectively.)[16] Most young Americans—the products of our schools and colleges—even if they chose to participate in the information revolution, would be utterly incapable of doing so. Likewise, and for the same reasons, they must get along without the consolations of traditional culture. Perhaps they are undertaking a sort of guerrilla rejection of literacy in general, whether print-based or digitalized; and perhaps their "radicalism" affords them certain satisfactions. In any case, they are refusing, or having refused for them, the skills that will be required if they are to choose for themselves the kind of life they want to have. And without that choice, the idea that this is a democracy becomes a sort of bitter joke.

Instead of undergoing a collapse, though, the economy is in a recovery, crash or no crash; and the social "contract" of democracy, however fictitious it may appear, continues to hold, insofar as it refers to the protection of property and the ordering of the work force. This leads Enzensberger to his conclusion that Western societies have institutionalized, de facto, an alternate representation of literacy, or illiteracy, as he refers to it—one that is truly, if ironically, "democratic":

> This new species is the second-order illiterate. . . . He has a talent for getting things done. We need have no worries about him. It contributes to the second-order illiterate's sense of well-being that he has no idea that he is a second-order illiterate. He considers himself well-informed; he can decipher instructions on appliances and tools; he can decode pictograms and checks. And he moves within an environment hermetically sealed against anything that might infect his consciousness. . . . An economy whose problem is no longer production but markets has no need of a disciplined reserve army of workers. The rigid training to which they were subjected also becomes redundant, and literacy becomes a fetter to be done away with. Simultaneous with the development of this problem, our technology has also developed an adequate solution. The ideal medium for the second-order illiterate is television. . . . It will become the rule to see second-order illiterates occupying the top positions in politics and business. In this connection, it is sufficient to indicate the current president of the United States. (P. 14)

It is Enzensberger's point that within the inflationary domain of media *coverage*, it is possible to be "well informed," to function effectively—even to represent the society in a political sense—and still to be an illiterate as regards "culture." In fact, such ignorance has become an asset, conferring a necessary dimension of spontaneity, of authenticity, upon the individual "communicator." Otherwise, college professors would be rich, and Americans in general would care as much about Matthew Arnold and Saul Bellow as they do about Bobby Ewing and Alexis Carrington.

Insofar as the university still functions representationally, what it represents is the piecemeal appropriation of individual culture by the colonial agents of media coverage. But this is no simple conquest—the replacement of one "consciousness" with another. Something more fundamental is taking place. The modernist economy of representation, by which a unitary consciousness is constituted, and which has informed the academy at least since Pater, is literally being dissolved. Not so that it can be replaced with something else, however, some collective, playful ideal such as Marx and even Derrida, for example, imagined. But so that such replacement will become impossible, and so that consciousness hereafter will be a restricted acquisition, just like literacy. Reflecting on another conquest—the European conquest of North America—Tzvetan Todorov has made the following, relevant observation:

> In order to speak of forms and kinds of communication, I have first of all adopted a typological perspective: the Indians favor exchanges with the world, the Europeans exchanges between men. . . . I have been led to observe an evolution in the "technology" of symbolism; this evolution can be reduced, for simplicity's sake, to the advent of writing. Now, the presence of writing favors improvisation over ritual, just as it makes for a linear conception of time or, further, the perception of the other.[17]

Something like the conquest of text over ritual is going on now, except in reverse. The literate individual—the individual of writing, linearity, improvisation—is being colonized by agents that would replace these forms with ritual and a mystified conception of identity.

As Enzensberger suggests, one has only to think of the presidential discourse (and the popularity of the "great communicator" who produces it) to grasp what is taking place. A knowledge of history, even a simple understanding of facts, often has little to do with the ritualized formulations of America's position and our mythical opposition to the Soviet Other, the "Evil Empire." Not surprisingly, then, such pulp myths as *Star Wars* and *Rambo* become sources of language and political intelligence. And our leaders are anything but introspective or thoughtful. Instead, they "favor exchanges with the world," as Todorov put it; they concern themselves with what they can learn from "the polls," which reflect opinions formulated by people whose values are determined, as theirs are, by the momentary intelligence of television, so that the president doesn't grow less popular for his obvious illiteracy; on the contrary, he was reelected by one of the largest margins in modern political history, which ought to come as no surprise, since he is a genuinely representative American.

As a representative, then, he represents nothing so much as the second-order individual, the successful colonial of the information revolution. From an academic standpoint, at least, there is no reason to expect opposition either to such representations or to the illiteracy for which they stand, because the faculties of culture are in complete disarray. A sort of institutional Alzheimer's disease has set in. There is no coherent consciousness—no ideology—that represents the individual of first-order literacy, or even the memory of such an individual, in relation to the larger institutional structure. What is more, there is no reason to assume that such representation will become either necessary or desirable. Within the academic space, a common language—or, more accurately, the expectation that language can and should communicate commonly intelligible meanings, regardless of the disagreements that may follow upon such communication—has long since been displaced (and debased) by the babble of mutually frustrating and nonreferential jargons (some for students, some for professors, some for administrators). Similarly, academic work has become an inflated, disciplinary inanity forced upon those, whether students or faculty, who are in no position to protest. Institutionally, there is nothing to be held, or represented, in common, for or against; there is no stage upon which the academic representation can be meaningfully addressed. All that we've got is the open lie of culture, so that the "life" of the university becomes a piece of bitter nonsense, just as with the Alzheimer's patient whose experience of consciousness has dwindled to painful, unrelated confrontations with things that he/she can no longer do. Within this entropic domain, info-colonization reduces a former community of interests—however arbitrary and contentious—to overlapping, and unrelated, service sites. I don't mean to sound nostalgic for a lost coherence: everybody's believing, or saying they believed, the same thing. In that connection, culture may once have worked, ideologically (regardless of how many people actually believed in it), but it also silenced more voices than it empowered. So now we've done culture in, through a combination of bad faith and deconstruction. But what we get in return is not liberation. Just the reverse.

Academics have found it impossible to account for our situation, except as such accounts are dictated to us, in a language not really and believably our own—one compounded of statistics and bureaucratic jargon. By so casually and uncritically dismissing the problematic of culture, or else delivering it into the hands of a neo-logistic, deconstructive technocracy, we have sacrificed our institutional history. (This much I am willing to concede to Hirsch and Bloom, despite their revivalist sensibilities.) If there is to be resistance to info-colonization, it's difficult to imagine where that resistance may come from, what experience will retain sufficient, representational authority to confront and call into question what is now going on. Culture surely won't do, since it is effectively dissipated, which is Bloom's point. So what then? The representational structure of the academy is being reduced—literally—to posthistorical fragments, none of which is capable of producing a consciousness of the whole.

However, on the face of things, the pseudo politics of crisis seems to have inspired a new sense of common cause in academic institutions, and the way they respond to the economy of work. According to a survey conducted by the American Council on Education, for example, more than 80 percent of all colleges and universities are either currently reviewing, or else have recently completed reviews of, new general education requirements,[18] presumably in an attempt to meet the challenge represented by such reports as that prepared by the American Association of Colleges, which concluded: "As for what passes as a college curriculum, almost anything goes. We have reached a point at which we are more confident about the length of a college education than its content and purpose."[19] By exposing the student to a "general education," it is to be expected, presumably, that she/he will come to understand the coherence and inherent meaningfulness of the baccalaureate experience—something which as yet eludes individual faculty members. And it will continue to elude them so as long as we cancel legitimate differences of opinion and the experience of historical confrontations with devalued, and devaluing, jargons, whether bureaucratic or theoretical.

Quite reasonably, language becomes the focus of such efforts to institute a serviceable, "general" idiom, or consciousness, by which an informational student might represent himself/herself coherently in relation to the greater, external sociality—just as the student of culture did a century ago. Consequently writing assessment has become the single most important method for measuring the work accomplished by academic instruction. According to the American Council on Education, more than 80 percent of "college leaders" consider this an appropriate measure of success, which is reflected in the fact that students are twice as likely to be assessed on the basis of their writing as any other criterion.[20] And since writing is almost always the exclusive province of English departments, it would seem that the agents of culture—however intentionally or advisedly—have been returned to prominence "across the curriculum." And their prominence is only likely to increase, given the drive for higher standards (and consequently more required remediation) combined with the levels of illiteracy pervasive among young people.

However, even if one wanted a return to *culture*—which I do not—that would be impossible. Whatever "college leaders" may think or say, the institution already represents the aftereffects of service colonization, and nowhere more so probably than in the domain of language, or writing. To begin with, the move toward standardized assessment indicates neither coherence nor success; it merely shows that the "problem" of remediation has been moved out of the public schools, where there are relatively strict standards governing the training and licensing of teachers, and into colleges and universities, where there are effectively no state or federal minimum requirements. Regardless of public breast-beating over the "failure" of the schools, this transfer of remediation is not likely to be opposed, since colleges are in need of students (thanks to the shrinking birthrate and the declining percentage of young people who choose to attend). Remedial classes not only provide head count, they also prolong a student's overall stay in college, making them a profitable investment of faculty time, particularly given the bargain-rate, part-time "faculty" who usually teach such courses.

As we have seen earlier, these "service providers" are no different from their nominal academic colleagues. On the contrary, their credentials and their aspirations, at least potentially, are the same: except that they failed at some point to receive preferment and must now make their fortunes in the academic colonies—the abandoned wilderness of the basic skills classroom, where nobody with a "real" career ever spends time. According to one estimate, 60 percent of all academic hiring done in "core" humanities fields in 1982–83 was at a non-tenure-track level.[21] These are the instructors, presumably, being hired in response to crisis, and who are being charged with frontline responsibilities in the "war" for quality education. Their plight is often talked about in journals such as *College English*, but that doesn't seem to change things very much. Part-time and non-tenurable hirings remain the fastest-growing part of the faculty in all types of institutions.[22] Not all these people, obviously, go to work in English departments to teach writing courses, but a good number of them surely do. And if present trends continue, ever more such instructors will be required, as increasing numbers of people— both postadolescents and working adults—find themselves in need of credentials in second-order (il)literacy, and as institutions find themselves in need of personnel to administer the "proficiency" curriculum devised in response.

The question is, What sort of proficiency is being taught and what quality of experience results? Both are important matters because the memory of what goes on under the comprehensive guise of "core" instruction must either define a consciousness—both institutional and individual—on which to base an account of *situation*; or else it must fail to live up to this announced, and frequently repeated, aim, thereby exposing both student and institution to unassimilable, though perhaps serviceable, exploitation. My argument is that the academy doesn't even attempt to address itself to the question of what its representations stand for, except as an invocation of powerless, cultural myths; and in so doing, it becomes a mere continuation of the colonial project for which potential illiterates are—however fortunately—being prepared. The object of attack, or dissolution, is the specific type of memory associated with first-order literacy—the sort of memory required to situate an individual, ideologically, in relation to a social and historical context. And that kind of memory is now rendered impossible within the institution, thanks to field-coverage specialization; likewise it is denied to students, who will never be confronted with, or by, their situation because the academic structure renders such representation impossible.

As regards colonial opportunities, the advantages of such a breakdown are obvious because where there is no memory, there can be no opposition to the second-order overtures of information. Even the deconstructionist "punks" of academe could not hope to compete, performatively, with the instantaneous hype of MTV; and in the *absence* of some external signified, such "pure and unrelated presents" will define the basis for the postreferential war of attention.[23]

The expressions of this breakdown—in terms of institutional literacy—are two, the one involving personnel and the other involving instructional materials. As to instruction, a recent publication of the federal government is indicative: *What Works: Research about Teaching and Learning*. Although the proximate audience is public-school parents and teachers, the booklet sets out what might be considered a general program of second-order illiteracy, beginning with the following statement by the president: "In assembling some of the best available research for use by the American public, *What Works* exemplifies the type of information the Federal government can and should provide."[24] Of particular interest is the section dealing with writing, which begins with the general advice that "the most effective way to teach writing is to teach it as a process of brainstorming, composing, revising, and editing" (p. 26). Whatever the validity of this "research finding," it at least represents the process-oriented approach practiced in most comp classrooms—an approach that either leaves out, or else leaves to the elective care of "real" teachers, the written record of the "culture." In the government pamphlet, for example, "writing" appears in a different section entirely from such topics as "history" and "cultural literacy," as if these were categorically, and necessarily, distinct. There is no discussion of "literature" at all. In college catalogs the same separation of topics and faculties obtains, particularly at the level of "requirements."

What happens, then, is that the student is required to undertake numerous rehearsals of the "writing process," beginning with grade school and culminating in the completion of college proficiency requirements. By that time he or she will have developed—in "compositions," group assignments, journal entries—a carefully articulated version of self as interpreted by the institution, and through the institution, in relation to society at large. (Either this will happen, or else the student will fail, and then be abandoned by both institution and educated society.) The student will also have developed a certain understanding of written language and what it is good for. The problem is that the whole "process" leads not to enlightenment but to triviality.

To begin with, if students are repeatedly asked to write out of "experience," the schools end up merely reproducing the content of second-order culture. The problem is not merely that such content is endlessly, and pointlessly, "processed"; it is the forms such processing takes. Typical of the agenda built into writing courses, and productive of the attitude that students assume toward their written presentation of self, is the format of a best-selling textbook for which I recently received a promotional flyer:

THE WRITING PORTFOLIO
    Writing to Express
        Writing the Personal Experience Essay/Writing the
            Personal Perspective Essay
    Writing to Tell
        Writing the How-To Essay/Writing the Problem-Solution
            Essay/Writing the Information Essay
    Writing to Change
        Writing the Assertion-With-Evidence Essay/Writing the
            Evaluation Essay/Writing the Persuasion Essay[25]

As per this outline, students begin with a recounting of what they did on their summer vacations, and they end with a five-page paper in favor of/opposed to gun control, abortion, prayer in the public schools, capital punishment, and so on, and so on. Some of them—the hopelessly naïve ones—may believe that at a later time, outside of school, they will be asked to do this sort of thing again. (They're the ones headed for the greatest disillusionment.) The cleverer ones, who remember reading a newspaper or watching a television program, or the ones who have had adult experience with writing as part of a job, know that the process of school literacy refers to nothing other than itself, just as the raving of schizophrenics—though often highly dramatic—remains nonsense.

Unlike true madness, the result of school assignments—the "autobiography" of pseudo consciousness that school institutes—is incredibly boring, as anyone knows who has ever read such essays, or been made to write them. Which is doubtless why so much attention is paid to the graphic design of books like the one described above. People must be amused, whether teachers or students, and the one thing second-order illiterates understand is pictures. Even the flyer is beautiful, therefore, and expensively produced, with tasteful photographs of the sunny Southwest, which are taken from the book itself:

> Stunning four-color photo essay
>
> —This introductory essay depicts the building of an adobe house from bare earth to finished product and draws an analogy between constructing a house and writing an essay. It illustrates beautifully the text's message—how to make something from nothing through the process of creation, development, and completion. (P. 4)

This description "illustrates beautifully" the problem with such an approach, as well as the reason why it fits so nicely in the space left by the failure of culture. It is not only the message of this text, but the message of all such texts and the curriculum based on them, that the aim of institutional writing is "to make something from nothing." And as any reasonable person knows, a representational product, such as language, is only as valuable as its reference, so that both the process of writing and the institutional subject to whom it refers are worth nothing, except within the arbitrary "house" of rules—a place where "nothing" is real.

However arbitrary Arnold's "touchstones" may have been, the forms of literacy based on them—both written and spoken—could be exchanged, for symbolic or ideological profit, in the larger space of the culture. There is at present no *culture* in relation to which one can assume such a meaningful position. As I suggested, however, it is not merely the "content" of writing courses that is implicated but also the instructional personnel—the largely unregulated, and even unknown, individuals—who comprise the language "faculty" of many universities, particularly large, state-supported institutions such as the one where I work, which are associated historically with preparing individuals for middle-class lives and careers. Statistically, about 60 percent of my colleagues are hired on a part-time or term basis, so that the majority of the English teachers are constituted, semester by semester, like the essays they teach, "out of nothing"—nothing, that is, as far as the received narrative of a "profession" is concerned.

Representationally, therefore, the memory of language that the institution has installed is primarily short-term. And it is to this mnemonic faculty that virtually every student who passes through the institution is exposed, since the proportion of nonpermanent teachers is usually equivalent to the number of "required" (that is to say, non-literature) courses offered by the department. At my school, for example, a student can complete a writing requirement (from remediation to advanced courses) as well as general education courses with a newly enhanced writing component and never once see a "real" faculty member. I doubt this situation is unique.

Whether or not this makes any difference is another question, although given the crisis-driven curriculum that "we" have elected, one person is probably as good as another at teaching the emptiness of language. For that matter, a person with no permanent institutional affiliation is probably better at the schizophrenic discourse of process illiteracy, or at least a more authentic representative. My present concern, however, is not for the effect on students but for the memory of institutions, or rather for its loss, because without a coherent awareness of what has happened, nothing is likely to change, for anybody.

As to what the result may be, that depends on which people and which institutions are concerned. "There are signs that America is becoming a more divided society," as Barbara Ehrenreich has recently remarked: "Over the last decade, the rich have been getting richer; the poor have been getting more numerous, and those in the middle do not appear to be doing as well as they used to."[26] If that is true, then the individuals who expect middle-class lives (which is still most Americans) and the institutions that teach them, or their teachers, must begin taking apart the social contract on which the past was founded. People must be taught, in other words, to expect less, or at least differently: the "text" of self must be rewritten so as to eliminate certain narrative habits of expectation and fulfillment that have grown anachronistic and potentially troublesome. Already the institution represents, collectively, an "individual" disabused of burdensome habits of memory.

In that connection the academy—like the individuals it serves— is becoming a second-order illiterate. The "faculties" of cultural memory have been essentially sequestered. Whatever "required" contacts there must be with the real world are conducted by short-term agents whose experience leaves no permanent trace on the institutional consciousness. Something worth attending to is going on here, something that affects all the interests the university represents: work, culture, language, the memory of history. Yet by surrendering to illiteracy, the institution merely provides an ivy cover for the dissolution of habits and traditions that it nominally preserves, just as the information "revolution" attacks the very class on whose labor it is founded. What is being eliminated, structurally, from institutions as from individuals, is the specific confrontations of memory with experience out of which a consciousness of situation might develop.

The point, then, is not to get further *out* of the culture, or what is left of it, but to learn how to get back into things: to admit, in other words, that "disinterestedness" is a value, a legitimation of knowledge, no longer appropriate to academic practice in the present class situation. The point is to refuse the discourse of emptiness, the marketable figure of unreality. At the same time, it is not desirable that the university, in an attempt at intelligence or coherence, should become an extension of the totalizing aims of politics or media coverage, though that temptation is clearly offered us. Crisis makes fearful demands for a return to some lost order, which like Arnold's *culture* was possible only at the price of enforced, mass exclusion, the withholding of language from experience, the cancellation of lived history. Somewhere between madness and terror, between illiteracy and evil, it would be nice to think that the academy, and those who work in it, still have a role.

6. Subjects

We fail for lack of an adequate subject. If there is to be an end to failure, then that's where we have to begin, with a consideration of subjects. After all the program areas are "covered" and all the sections staffed, there is still no subject that the representative agents of the university might hold in common, regardless of whether they agree or disagree after reaching that common ground. If the subject is to be *literacy*, of whatever order, then most professors have little or nothing to do with the practical life of their institutions since they avoid the departments and committees where it is invoked. And when literacy does get discussed, it is usually in the context of remediation or service: "basic" instruction such as would be a waste of expensive, "regular" faculty time. Not a job for professionals, according to the popular wisdom. If the subject of the university is to be *literature*, as the presiding vocabulary of culture would lead one to believe, then most students never get a look at what we *really* do (and what the university as a whole ostensibly stands for) since comparatively few of them return electively to the liberal arts after their "basic" (which is to say, nonliterary) requirements are met. And even if they do, they are no more likely to encounter a recognizable subject there, within the evacuated space of the academic classroom, where no real work ever takes place. Instead, what they get are hollow, disciplinary rituals that trivialize language and labor alike, and that remain nontransferrable, whether from class to class, or from school to the real world.

For lack of a practical subject, then, it remains impossible to

117

talk together—all of us, whether in or out of the liberal arts, whether we're on the same side or on different ones—about what is going on, so that most of the time, we really don't know, nor could we be expected to explain it to somebody else. Not that it makes much difference because the failure of the university, though everybody's business, is nobody's fault. In effect, the people with real jobs work for themselves, writing the articles and books that no student (and few "colleagues") will ever read. Part-timers and grad students aren't similarly self-employed, obviously, but they aren't implicated either, any more than the aspiring actor who waits tables in the Broadway deli is responsible for the lousy corned beef. Like the actor they don't really work here; they're just hanging on, looking for their big break. And as to administrators, how can they be expected to administer subjects that professional academics are incapable of identifying?

Not only is there an absence of a subject for all of us to teach, in whatever different or confrontive ways, there is an absence of subject in the sense that we never think or talk about who is being taught, about the kind of individual we collectively stand for, given the disparate representations of the faculty. Rather, discussions of curriculum always end up a subject-less proxy fight in behalf of vested interests. Colleges, departments, programs must all scramble to hold onto their piece of the action, their share of the available headcount, though we talk very little about what goes inside the heads we are counting and whether or not it, all together, makes any sense. Which leads people like Secretary Bennett to conclude that we don't know what we're doing. And of course he's right. But he's not right in presuming that the dead coherence of culture offers a viable solution. For people—academics—who already feel set upon from all sides, he's just one more piece of bad news, albeit one "written" in a recognizable idiom. Control is everywhere, but nobody seems to be in charge.

It should come as no surprise, then, that academics find themselves attracted to the prison, both actually and metaphorically; and particularly to the powerful, and frequently romantic, representations of Michel Foucault. He fills up with dark conspiracy the void that our absence of subject creates. In place of petty politics, he offers the vicarious titillations of *power*, albeit somebody else's. I'm no better than the next humanist, so a few years back I decided to literalize my critical situation. I taught college classes in prisons— an experience I look back on as both quixotic and instructive. For my first class—a class funded, appropriately, by the National Endowment for the Humanities—I asked the students to read some

Foucault. I'd hoped to build a bridge between the prisoners and me. We, all of us, live and work inside institutions, I told them; we exist, we are "written," as subjects of state surveillance; and so on, and so on. That was several years ago, as I said, when people seemed more inclined to talk about the university, and society generally, in terms of "discipline and punishment." In some ways this analysis was valid, and still is, despite the hysteria and stupidity often perpetrated on its behalf. But when it comes to academic life, the subject of discipline misses one crucial distinction, which my students the inmates were quick to point out. The jail they lived in was one they wanted to get out of; the one I kept talking about—the university— was one that I was working very hard to remain within. (Besides, who but an insider could read Foucault anyhow?) And that makes all the difference in the world.

Even so, it is still too soon to forget Foucault, despite the advice of Jean Baudrillard; it's too soon because he offers a subject—albeit a wrong one—too powerful to be ignored. One reason, perhaps, why it is tempting to forget him is that his discourse has so effectively passed into the domain of assumed truth, at least among dispirited liberal-arts types. We all *know* we work inside the panopticon; we *know* we are subject to the interrogation and surveillance of power. Or what would be more accurate to say, we know we *want* to work inside an institution where our importance and value are such that somebody is always watching us. We no longer have to be told, whether we share those views or not. In either case they largely dictate the professional representation of the university, its rhetorical reality. Now, why we should surrender to so unenviable a position is another matter, which is not very well understood. In general I think academics, particularly academics whose area of study is the humanities, react as I did when I prepared for my first visit to the prison. I needed to feel as real to myself as I imagined the convicts to be; and whatever feeling I was looking for I didn't find in the professional study of my subject, literature, at least not in the way I understood it. But as the subject of Foucault's disciplinary narcissism, I began to feel "better" about myself, more significant, and in a position to meet the prisoners on their own ground.

Of course, what my feeling masked is the basic lie on which this posture is founded: I worked for the institution, and they lived inside it; I would give out the grades, and they would receive them. At least my feelings were honest, though, like I expect the feelings of my colleagues to be when they affect a cynical disdain of administrators and faculty politics as if posthistorical irony could somehow immunize them against the unreality they feel and put them in touch with something more authentic. Or if not that, at least spare them the embarrassment of appearing still to believe in culture. Better the austere insularity of Foucault, or the eternal, admonitory recess of Derridean free play. But regardless of how playful or insulated, the pseudo subject thus compounded knows nothing at all—certainly not anything worth professing. At best, he/she merely sympathizes with a situation over which all control and responsibility have been fortuitously and conveniently relinquished; and that only serves to maintain the emptiness of academic representations.

So, as Count Tolstoy used to say, what then must we do? My answer is that if the subject we've got doesn't work, or doesn't even exist, then we need a new one. To begin with, if there is to *be* a common subject, that subject can be conceived only in relation to something that we are all actually and believably subject to. For such purposes the academic institution will not do, since it contains so many different classes of subjects, some allied, others in opposition; and its superficiality is such that few people, except for the professors, probably feel it is real anyhow, Foucault notwithstanding. Nor will the macro subject of the state suffice, and for a similar reason. It is nonsense to talk about "us," for instance, without first talking about the differences of race and sex and class that constitute the lives "we" lead. And as far as the state is concerned, these differences will never yield a common subjectivity. Instead, I want to propose *literacy* as our common subject, though not the accidental literacy currently installed in the college curriculum, and not the truncated literacy characteristic of Enzensberger's second order.

What I have in mind is a literacy based on collaborative enterprise and constructive confrontation. I want to propose literacy as a postcultural stage on which we might animate the subject of our common differences and disagreements. But if such a literacy is to become possible, it's the academics who must make the first move. After all, the second-order practitioners—and their acolytes—are already out there, and doing very well without us. If academics are to become literate, then the first thing that must happen is the withering of "the professor," since it is this role—bound up with an exhausted, historical subjectivity—that prevents us from imagining our subject differently. Not that this has always been so. On the contrary, the professor—as opposed to the gentleman of culture—was a necessary figural invention. If the study of language was to be organized and institutionalized effectively, practitioners needed some means of reproducing themselves professionally. Medicine and the law had already accomplished this by the end of the nineteenth century. What was required for college teachers was an organization that would institute uniform quantitative standards of admission (with reference to specific university curricula), and so displace the qualitative, informal, and largely closed admission standards of the gentleman practitioners. Under the aegis of the Modern Language Association, then, language study emerged as a profession, as I have already explained. The other humanities have subsequently followed suit in instituting themselves professionally. The professor, however, is no less a historical—and historically limited—subject than the gentleman whom he replaced.

The anachronistic professor now prohibits our recognizing a subject that is not merely hypothetical but real, although this reality is little credited among us. If the yearly surveys of freshman attitudes conducted by the *Chronicle of Higher Education* can be believed, students wish, more than ever, to identify themselves with the life of visible success (and frequent excess) presided over by our ambiguous mascot, the Yuppie. The new info-serv economy is booming, with the Dow Jones industrial average up more than 500 points over the last two years (even after the crash); Americans feel considerable confidence, economically speaking, with consumer spending running on average 26 percent ahead of actual growth.[1] Obviously some people know how to make things work, how to read the future; and these days they are usually not ashamed of displaying the material signs that identify a literate life(style). That is Enzensberger's point, which is likely to become more, rather than less, potent thanks to the uncertainty of current markets and the consequent wish to cling, however fearfully, to the talismans of success. Not surprisingly, given the traditional role of colleges in presiding over entry into middle-class careers, students arrive expecting that this is the place to find out how to get on in the world, how to become literate in the ways of, and profitably subject to, a postindustrial future, which now more than ever depends upon the pervasive modeling of language. What they usually find, however, is not literacy but illiteracy, at least as far as the actual subject of this society is concerned. Even in practical fields such as business, there is no meaningful consciousness of subject because discussions remain bound by the exhausted discourse of culture.

This "message" provides the comic material for Rodney Dangerfield's film *Back to School*, in which he plays the character Thornton Melon, who has made himself a millionaire selling outsized ready-to-wear in his chain of Tall and Fat stores. Now, somewhat past mid-

life, Melon, who never got to college the first time around, returns
to school along with his teenage son. What he discovers, comically,
is that there is no place in the academic system for nontraditional
students like him; there is no way to take seriously what he knows,
whether in business courses or in his literature class; and he is not
willing to create himself an illiterate merely for the purpose of getting
an education. The academy, it seems, is incapable of recognizing—
much less crediting—an authentic subject.

As I have already pointed out, a non-comic version of this same
refusal comes in *The Closing of the American Mind: How Higher
Education Has Failed Democracy and Impoverished the Souls of
Today's Students*, by Allan Bloom, and *Cultural Literacy: What
Every American Needs to Know*, by E. D. Hirsch, Jr.[2] Within weeks
of their publication, these books had risen to the number one and
number two slots respectively on the *New York Times* list of best-
sellers. The emphasis differs in each case. Hirsch is concerned more
with specific knowledge, and with the failure of the schools to turn
out culturally literate Americans; Bloom is worried about a general
failure of spiritual courage, which he sees exemplified in the poor job
that American colleges and universities do in teaching the classics.
In both instances, however, the authors' strategy is the same. They
invoke a now familiar crisis and galvanically resuscitate the cadaver
of culture, in order to remind the public of how valuable education
is, or ought to be. Their point, then, is anticipated by Rodney Dangerfield, who had already demonstrated the distance separating institutional literacy from the practical literacy that characterizes a
culture of informational as well as economic inflation. The difference
is that in the film the faculty and Thornton Melon both change; they
collectively "write" a new, collaborative subject, more in keeping
with the lives of real men and women. And everything works out
happily. That is not the case for Bloom and Hirsch; comedy is not
their concern.

For them, and particularly for Bloom, it may already be too
late, which is the point of his unselfconsciously ironic title, *The
Closing of the American Mind*. Insofar as Bloom's university represents "the American mind," that mind is surely closed. He advo-
cates a return to the Great Books, urging the following on their behalf:
"Men may live more truly and fully in reading Plato and Shakespeare
than at any other time, because then they are participating in essential
being and are forgetting their accidental lives" (p. 380). Although he
is surely correct in saying that the curricula of most colleges represent
mere confusion and political expediency, he does the classics no

favor by setting them up in so ridiculous an opposition: essential being versus accidental reality; truth versus life; gown versus town.

The same impulse guides Hirsch, who provides a sixty-page appendix at the end of his book, "What Literate Americans Know." The appendix is just a list of names, dates, and phrases that supposedly characterize cultural literacy. Following are some of the listings for *c*-words:

> charisma
> Charlemagne
> Charles I (Great Britain)
> Charleston (dance)
> Charleston, South Carolina
> Charleston, West Virginia
> Charlotte, North Carolina
> Charon
> Chartres, cathedral of
> Chattanooga, Tennessee
> Chaucer, Geoffrey
> chauvinism
>   (P. 162)

Perhaps the most interesting thing about this list—aside from its presiding close-mindedness—is its fetishizing of technology—specifically, the historically bound technology of print-based culture, which is exclusively the source of Hirsch's quiz.

The same list, or kind of list, could have been drawn up at any time since the invention of movable type. Technologically, Hirsch—like Bloom—is unwilling to take seriously, as forms of decisive, cultural literacy, anything but the printed word; or any cultural form that resists reduction to discursive précis. He is unconcerned, for example, with the forms of image and sound production, not to mention the pervasive commercial culture that characterizes contemporary American society. Where is Marilyn Monroe's face, for instance, or the opening bars of the "Star Spangled Banner"? Or for that matter, what about Charlie the Tuna? If the point of cultural literacy is the effective sharing of information and experience, I expect the phrase "Sorry, Charlie," would get you a lot further—even among college English professors—than an allusion to the cathedral at Chartres; and it surely has a lot more to do with the role that language plays in our lives, whether good or ill. Perhaps—just perhaps—people stop knowing things that no longer matter to them. And if the university, and particularly the humanities, are to have any impact on the experience of contemporary Americans, they serve themselves ill by identifying with *absence*: with the myriad things that people don't know, or else gave up caring about. The appeal to great traditions, at this point, is perhaps attractive, but also absurd. If Matthew Arnold, for instance, were to read either Bloom's or Hirsch's book, I expect he would find the authors little better than heathens, since neither demands a knowledge of Latin and Greek as the foundation of real literacy. And as any gentleman knows, one reads the classics only in the original language.

My point is not to advocate a new "relevance," or to affiliate the academy with John Naisbitt's "high touch" mutation of culture. I am glad, for the most part, that we have been spared the necessities of what Arnold referred to as the "practical" view of things. At the same time, I think the presiding figure of crisis, such as that invoked by Bloom and Hirsch, invites a particularly dangerous way of thinking, for people both inside and outside the academy. A literacy constituted on the absence of subject will find more and more to make itself absent from. In that connection, the "success" of both books is a far from happy sign. Rather, it confirms a taste among literate readers—who are the only likely audience—to think of themselves and what they know as somehow forgotten by, and irrelevant to, the practical view. And in this connection, the separation that Arnold valued is not so good a thing.

What I hope, instead, is that the academy, and particularly literature professors, might begin to take seriously the multiform literacy that exists: not instead of their own but concurrent with it. After all, the professor shares with everyone else the wash of words and images and auditory cues that constitutes contemporary experience. In this relation, Enzensberger falsely assumes a separation between first- and second-order literacy. This may be true from the standpoint of the second-order illiterate, but it is surely not the case the other way around. The professor has no choice but to be present in the second-order world, regardless of how seriously she/he takes it. After all, the professor finds her/his life in this world: votes in it, consumes in it, propagates in it, fantasizes in it, and finally shares responsibility for it, both good and ill. The literacy that gets the professor and everybody else around—with either more or less success and intelligence—is the basis of a boom economy and rapid technological developments in the new domain of info-serv. At the same time, this literacy characterizes a society with the largest prison population in American history, a society where 60 percent of the people feel alienated from the power structure (up from 29 percent in 1966), where 81 percent of the population feel that the rich get richer and the poor get poorer. And, statistically speaking, they are right, particularly if the people involved happen to be blacks or women (Harris, pp. 33–35). Any literacy, so-called, that does not engage the texts generated by this society is at best a joke and at worst a threat.

Surely no intelligence deserves the name *liberal* when it so casually dismisses as "vulgarity" or "accident" the whole domain— of spectacular efficiency, genius, and profligacy—that lies outside the university common. It is the worst sort of demagoguery for the people who know the most about the study of language—most of whose careers depend upon public money—to adopt a willful igno- rance as to the role that language plays in the lives of their fellow citizens. We needn't give up Shakespeare and Plato, but we ought to think of them not as the possessions of a hypothetical and *absent* subject but as the actual knowledge of a real one. If the real world is truly out there, in other words, what place do they have in it? How might one be subject to both past and present, sacrificing neither to the superior claims of "culture"? Academics, obviously, don't know the answer—at least, not when it comes to *their* institutionalized past. That's why they get so angry and accusatory when other people ask the question, or what is worse, when our pastiche-loving "pop- ular" culture plunders the past without their permission.

We spend too much time fetishizing textual objects and too little wondering about our subject. How would one begin to teach a course, for instance, in practical literacy? That's what Shakespeare had in mind when he dressed his Romans in Elizabethan costumes and let them speak London vernacular. He wasn't writing history; nor did he care about mere popularization. He was making news; that was his subject. Maybe it should be ours too. At least, it's a question worth asking.

Academics, however, for all their Socratic vanity, seem little given to questions of this sort. Because of a failure of nerve or imagination, or both, we fall back on the panoptic cliché of "the institution" to excuse us, to cover for our indifference and compla- cency. But this is an institution that *we* invented and maintain, and one that we could change. Most important, this is not merely an academic matter. As with the previous rationalization of the assembly line, there is an analogous process going forward in the info-serve economy. The level of skills required to get by is getting lower (which is the implied point of both Bloom's and Hirsch's analysis); but the level of skills required to manipulate technology is much higher, particularly with regard to language skills. As a result, the middle level of skill—like that of the skilled craftsman before—is simply withering. Heretofore people who found themselves caught might look to colleges and universities to provide what they needed, to place them in a position of choosing their life. Without such options democracy is meaningless. Increasingly, though, what such people find when they come to us is the same withdrawal of prospects, the same melting of the middle class, that characterizes their life situation. But this need not be the case, for the reasons I have suggested. If we took seriously the subject that is actually at hand, we might perhaps have a humanities worthy of the name.

Here tradition has left the academy stranded, so that progress— if there is to be any—must come through nontraditional means. This is why the present situation, though difficult, is not hopeless, because the one resource of which the academy is in no short supply is nontraditional clients and unprecedented circumstances. If we were ever to decide to take seriously the notion of a new subject, and to devise particular offerings to go with it, we would be in excellent company, since such an undertaking would require the precise store of practical, adult experiences that we now have at hand, what with the influx of mid-life retrainees. I don't mean inventing some course like "Shakespeare for Middle Managers," or "George Eliot and Geopolitics"; we've had enough of that stuff already. In any case, such courses (like the supposedly new "core curriculum") serve only as vehicles for the same teachers to give the same lectures they always give, except for a few contemporizing souvenirs. The point is to make it impossible for the old literacy to keep on working, institutionally, just as it has quit working in the real world. A new subject might invite an examination of both failures and make it possible to imagine a literacy that would be critical of past as well as present, without holding the shortcomings of the one against the other, and vice versa.

Given a different subject—literacy—education would not imply a necessary attack on the self-confidence of the student. If the point were to investigate a problem to which neither student nor teacher had the solution, then nobody could lay claim to superior authority. The subject of literacy thus constituted would provide a way to work within existing institutions without becoming an academic inmate who is merely doing time until her/his release. The academic class system supported by the division of labor ("real" work versus teaching, class work versus things that matter, research versus service) would cease if everybody concerned were working on the same thing; and if their work directly, critically engaged life experience, rather than nullifying it; and if it led them, critically, to engagement with each other. Intellectual discipline might be restored if the bad faith underlying the academy were done away with. Teachers wouldn't need to make up to the students, or to themselves, for things that they ostensibly didn't believe in but that they felt compelled to do anyhow.

The point is for the university to regain an ideological purchase on real life such as that implicit in Arnold's project of *culture*: to represent, honestly, the confrontations on which any institutional literacy is founded. In this connection, the pseudo-coherence that Hirsch and Bloom imply is just that. Barring organic complication, every human is literate in one way or other. Each of us is able, in a semiotic sense, to read and reproduce signs. For ideological purposes, however, different societies choose to value some forms of literacy and to devalue others, which means that illiterates are not found but made. They are made by literates who want to universalize their own chosen ways of doing things, or at least to universalize their ideological superiority. As to actual universality, that is probably not desirable, since it would dissolve the differences on which the exercise of power depends. This is intended not in way of revelation but as a statement of obvious facts.

Nevertheless, there is implied in current debates about literacy an incarnation of what might be called Diderot's dream—the encyclopedist fantasy that there exists such a thing as final knowledge toward which all minds naturally tend. This is clearly not the case, though not so clearly as to prevent the falsification of institutional representations of literacy, which have more in common with neoclassic rules than contemporary experience—ours or anybody else's. I hasten to add, however, that my aim is not to propose an academic anarchy to take the place of a superannuated culture. Rather I hope to represent the subject of literacy as it actually exists: as confrontations that can be studied in any number of different, and significant, ways: in terms of class, gender, race, historical situation, and so on. The point—if that is the right word—is *not* to settle, and thus falsify, literacy encyclopedically, so that its study becomes closed to nonacademicians who can only observe, but never hope to participate actively in, its formulation. Crisis or no crisis, a literacy not available for active participation is one that finally doesn't matter, as the recent peripheralizing of the liberal arts demonstrates.

At the same time, given the political *fact* of literacy—a fact well illustrated if not overtly expressed in the work (and instant prominence) of Hirsch, Bloom, Enzensberger, and company—everybody is not going to be right; all responses are not going to be treated equally. It is the worst kind of liberal idiocy to pretend this is so: no one believes it, and evidence to the contrary is everywhere. Difference, confrontation, then, ought to be the overt subject of our undertakings, rather than the canceled secret on which the academy bases its precarious, if presumptuous, power.

The problem is that very few people believe academic literacy is superior, or even equal, to real-world literacy. Nobody except for academics, that is, and even they aren't too sure or else the first bit of advice they hand out to people looking for outside jobs would be different; they wouldn't recommend hiding academic credentials. Faced with this situation, it is possible, of course, to adopt the monastic option (and to make the *Times* best-seller list by doing so): to retire to private contemplation while we let the second-order world go to hell in its illiterate, though often very comfortable, handbasket. More often than not, that is the option we, collectively—if passively—choose. But I think it's a wrong one, and needless, for the reasons I have explained. And if the figures about academic job satisfaction can be believed, it's not one that produces much happiness anyhow. So we ought to do something different, for our sakes and for everybody else's too. If those people "out there" really are illiterates, it's not their fault they don't know how deeply we care about their deprivation. When's the last time we sent them a message in language they could understand? Are they supposed to read Bloom's and Hirsch's books, for example? I doubt it. Those are for us: home diagnostic kits to confirm the terminal forebodings we already know too well.

Such changes as I have proposed may or may not ever take place. As to the likelihood, I defer to the comment of a student I taught once in prison. On his course evaluation, he wrote: "Your [*sic*] doing the best you can with what you have at hand to work with." He'd assumed—wrongly, as it turned out—that I was really working with what lay at hand. I was not, although I don't think I was aware of it at the time. The trick is to figure out how to see what is *there*, and how to value it: how to take real life seriously, in other words, so that the work done in its behalf can be undertaken with the same commitment and expectation of shared benefit as one might bring to the preparation of a meal. I expect I didn't want to see too much of what was going on in prison because of the implications. And anyhow, as far as the student was concerned, not much was likely to change; and he knew that. We have the prisons we want; and until we begin wanting something different, they'll stay the way they are: as close to hell as I hope I ever get. That's why I quit working there, because what I was doing was a lie. We have no wish to humanize that place, and we make it impossible for the people inside it to do so. For that matter, the inmates and guards—many of them—are prepared, institutionally, to literalize our culture of violence. They have little else to do and nothing to lose. But as the prisoners kept reminding me, our institutions—theirs and mine—are different; college is not jail. We only make it seem that way sometimes, to ourselves and our students, for reasons both fatuous and regrettable.

Conclusion

This is the place in books like mine where the practical advice usually appears. After the serious stuff is over, but before everybody heads for home, you play a couple of quick rounds of *what if* with your reader: not that it matters, because it really doesn't, but just in case you're wondering *what* would happen *if* I took any of the foregoing seriously, and so on. That's the implication, at least: that real life is an afterthought.

Once more, then, the problem of language and academic lying comes up, because if professors really did take seriously—as "we" claim to do—the crisis that supposedly threatens our every waking, institutional moment, the advice would come first, with the discursive rehashing of politics, positions, power being reduced to the status of an appendix, if there were time for such considerations at all. But, of course, that would mean a valuing of action over language production; and so long as the current economy of academic careers endures, action will remain generally irrelevant. I have yet to encounter, for instance, in any evaluation for tenure or promotion, a category of "good deeds"; on the other hand, "scholarship" (which is to say private writing published in little-read journals) is usually the first item of concern. What this means is that academics keep on doing what they do best, which is "talking" without either hope or threat of practical consequences. Nobody is supposed to take any of this seriously, except as language, which academic culture has effectively absolved of any ties to real life. Concurrently the academic bureaucracy is left to do what it does best, which is reproduce what

131

is already here. And if anybody asks questions, there's the devalued but still powerful script of culture, which we have been rehearsing, all of us, for more than a hundred years now.

This characterization obviously leads to a hopeless conclusion: things will never change. That is probably why action gets reduced to the position of trivial afterthought, because it seems so little likely that anything can or will be done. Admittedly, academics *do* often prefer talking/writing to acting, and bureaucrats *can* usually be counted upon to perform their job, which is to maintain the bureau. But in an academic institution, the opposition of language and action is a false one—at least in part—so that the seemingly inevitable conclusion of hopelessness is based on a faulty premise. The essential reality here *is* language; language is what the institution makes and, in turn, is made of. For academics language is *how we act*. Until that language has acquired a history—an objective situation—it is difficult to act meaningfully on its behalf, particularly when action will itself inevitably take the form of further language production. Which is to say that the talking must, of necessity, come before the doing. But language, of course, is not the only form of action. What I hope is that I have now situated the language of culture in such a way as to develop a consequent strategy for general action.

Having said this, I am led to Charles Dickens's conclusion that these are both the best and the worst of times. On the one hand, as I've suggested, it is possible to believe that nothing will ever change. Academics made the schools, and, for all their talking, they seem little inclined to change them. For that matter, we have turned crisis into a highly profitable cottage industry: witness the book you are reading now. On the other hand, since there is nothing to change but ourselves, the academy could be transformed overnight; and in most cases the "they" who eternally stand in the way of progress would have little or nothing to say about it. After all, we practice our profession in a space—the classroom—where nothing is real and where nobody is actually watching, so where would resistance come from? The answer, of course, is that resistance comes from within, although the voices that compel us to suffer and be still are not usually identified as our own. It is a matter of no small irony that language professionals appear incapable of speaking for themselves, except to confirm what everyone already knows, which is that academic work is irrelevant to the concerns of real life. By default, then, administrators do our public talking for us, using the hand-me-down script of culture, which they don't seem to believe in and which none of us pays much attention to any more either. But that's where the wonderful possibilities arise. If language is all there is holding this place—the university—together, then professionals whose only work is language are in a position of ultimate power.

We might begin by taking seriously the representational role of the institution—a role that history has saddled us with, like it or not. If work is what the university now represents, then we could start there: by working on the subject of literacy. As Henry Giroux has pointed out,

> Neither the emergent new public philosophy nor the old humanist version of the liberal arts provide a model for rethinking the purpose of liberal education. . . . A more suitable model can be developed around a public philosophy that links the purpose of higher education to the development of forms of knowledge and moral character in which citizenship is defined as an ethical compact, not a commercial contract, and empowerment is related to forms of self and social formation that encourage people to participate critically in shaping public life.[1]

Given this context, there are things to work for and things to work against; and it would be foolhardy to expect that all of "us" will ever agree as to just which is which. And that is a good thing because within the space defined by such confrontation, culture and the forms of literacy for which it stands might come to mean something real, something worth working for in the lives of the citizens of this republic.

The work I can imagine doing is of two sorts, or rather, it involves two dimensions of academic representation: one internal and the other external. And both implicate the academic valuation of language. The problems confronting the academy result from a disconnecting of inside and outside—culture and work, art and life—with the result that nothing real can go on here, least of all, work. Therefore, what has to be done is a reintroduction of inside to outside, "us" to "them." Such reconnecting depends, necessarily, on the specific medium—language—which sustains the university and academic careers, regardless of how scientific and/or "practical" those careers may be. Too often, however, this medium becomes the instrument of trivialization and undoing. We ought to take seriously the things that language does and the things we do with it. That is Derrida's point. What he does not invite is the confusion of *différance*, or free play, with a cynical absenteeism: the conviction, if *conviction* is the right word, that anything merely made of language has no real life, which can be referred to now only within the sneering enclosure of quotation marks, as if four spots of ink comprehended the project of deconstruction. For some people, of course, punctuation supplants intelligence.

Thirty years ago Raymond Williams saw pretty clearly what was coming: "Any practical denial of the relation between conviction and communication, between experience and expression," he said, "is morally damaging alike to the individual and to the common language."[2] As he went on to point out, however,

> It is certainly true, in our society, that many men, many of them intelligent, accept, whether in good or bad faith, so dubious a role and activity. The acceptance in bad faith is a matter for the law. . . . The acceptance in good faith, on the other hand, is a matter of culture. It would clearly not be possible unless it appeared to be ratified by a conception of society which relegates the majority of its members to mob-status. . . . This is the real danger to democracy. (P. 304)

And it is a danger that ought to be particularly felt, and represented, in the popular institutions of a democracy. But it isn't, or at any rate, not nearly enough.

The business of the academy—like that of a democracy—is confrontation, the popular representation of difference, though more often than not we use language to hide rather than reveal what we are about, whether in good faith or bad. That—confrontation—has been our historical situation, the origin of academic representations, at least since Matthew Arnold's "anarchists" tore down the railings in Hyde Park. Those people weren't asking for "relevance"; they couldn't have cared less about the melioration of a "core curriculum." They wanted action—specifically, political action—and if things weren't going to go their way, they wanted to know why, which prompted Arnold to his discovery of culture as an active opposition of memory and forgetting. They wanted to forget the past, and he wanted to forget the present. Regardless of what one feels about Arnold's formulations, he saw culture for what it is (potentially, at any rate): a space for staging the altogether serious work of language; not a "commercial contract," as Henry Giroux has said, but an "ethical compact" that "encourage[s] people to participate critically in shaping public life." That is the only context in which the problematic of culture has any meaningful possibility. Otherwise, it is reduced to being just one more text among many others, and not a very interesting text at that. Interesting or not, however, this text—unitary, repressive, lifted out of history—has too often ended up at the disposal of individuals prepared to write off the mass of society as merely a mob. The results for language, and the institutions attached to it, have been extreme.

If that is to change, such change might well begin with an assumption, or redefinition, of the university not as text but as cultural space within which the work of language—literacy of various sorts—is to go forward. Given that assumption, then, academics ought to write and speak as if they expected to be understood by society generally, because the topics under discussion are ones that matter. (One assumes that even "pure" researchers would not go so far as to argue for things that don't matter.) Similarly, the literacy of students ought to be modeled on the same expectation. Next, academics ought to put their language, if not themselves, into jeopardy. They ought to go to places where people could hear them and say what they think about culture, literacy, and academic work. I don't mean the dumb-show resorts of professional meetings, but the representational space of the university, to begin with, and also the community that the university supposedly serves and is supported by. And rather than pretending to a consensus that doesn't exist and probably never has existed, academics ought to "stage" the conflicts that make their questions—at least to professors—seem more than merely academic. As Gerald Graff has suggested, this could begin in the classroom, where students rarely if ever get to see the confrontations that animate professorial culture. If they, or anyone else, are to understand why academic problems matter, such confrontations must be made clear and understandable.[3]

In that connection, I want to end with an expression of respect, if not precisely admiration, for the work of William Bennett, Allan Bloom, and E. D. Hirsch. They have taken seriously the problem of academic culture; and they have written and spoken as if they believed what they have said, and believed in the potential of language—if not to get at the truth, at least to express an honest, and understandable, thought. And they have done this in the widest public arena. That's just the sort of thing that I think academics ought to be doing: not instead of their work, but as a legitimate expression of it. I am indebted to Hirsch in particular, so much so that I want to appropriate his idea of a "list" to my own purposes by way of conclusion. I also want to appropriate his proviso. The following is a list of things a person might do; I do not intend to "create a complete catalogue of American knowledge but to establish guideposts that can be of practical use to teachers, students, and all others who need to know our literate culture." That is more or less what I have in mind.

Appendix

Another List
Or, Things a Professor Might Do

1. Do a better job than the people who are messing up the university.
2. Tell your students which courses to take next semester, and why. If a colleague questions your recommendations, invite her/him to share a class with you. You teach your version of the course materials, then she/he does the same; then you discuss your differences. Since you would each be covering the other's class during the trade-off period, no new funding would be required. The schedule need not be changed. All that would be necessary is individual action. (This is Graff's idea of "staging.")
3. Invite students to write an academic autobiography: what the institution made me do, and why I do/don't like it. Express a low tolerance for lying.
4. Finish your book on universities, then run for some committees.
5. Encourage your friends to do the same. (If you've lost track of your friends in the last few months, phone them up.)
6. Whenever you write a paper for a professional meeting, try reading it to one of your classes. Watch the faces of your students, then ask yourself, "Is this trip really necessary?"
7. Hold a contest for best teacher, then announce as the prize that everybody will come by to watch the best teacher teach. See what happens.
8. Each fall stage a colloquium for incoming students and the uni-

versity community generally; invite your chair to explain why your subject matters.

9. Go to the meeting and disagree.
10. Read the introduction to your college catalog. If you agree with what it says about the value of a liberal education, make a copy and give it to your students. Tell them why you agree. If you don't agree, make a copy and give it to your students. Tell them why you disagree.
11. Take real life more seriously. Watch TV as if it mattered as much as John Milton.
12. Hide the lecture notes for the survey course you teach every fall; put them in a place where you'll forget them. Next fall, do something different.
13. Ask a local service club or organization if you can go to their next meeting and explain why people in your field are useful. Write a paper describing your answer. Read the paper to the service club. Then read it to the members of your department, unless you're a chicken.
14. Ask your students in each class to make a list of three things they'd rather be doing. Then ask them why they aren't doing those things.
15. You do the same thing, then explain your list.
16. Start a journal. Demand that all the articles be written in understandable English.
17. Make a list of your intellectual and/or professional adversaries; make a list of your allies. Show the lists to your students and explain who is on them and why.
18. Teach your intro class the wrong way one day. See if anybody notices. If they do, explain what you have done. If they don't, explain what you have done.
19. Remind everyone to read more Blake:

> Without Contraries is no progression.
> Prudence is a rich ugly old maid courted by Incapacity.
> He who desires but acts not, breeds pestilence.
> The cut worm forgives the plow.
> Dip him in the river who loves water.

Notes

Introduction

1. Allan Bloom, *The Closing of the American Mind: How Higher Education Has Failed Democracy and Impoverished the Souls of Today's Students* (New York: Simon & Schuster, 1987).
2. E. D. Hirsch, Jr., *Cultural Literacy: What Every American Needs to Know* (Boston: Houghton Mifflin, 1987). With this and all subsequent citations, page numbers after the first note will be included in the text.
3. T. S. Eliot, *Selected Prose of T. S. Eliot*, ed. Frank Kermode (New York: Harcourt Brace Jovanovich, 1975), p. 298.
4. See, for example, Helen Lefkowitz Horowitz's general debunking of academic golden ages in *Campus Life: Undergraduate Cultures from the End of the Eighteenth Century to the Present* (New York: Knopf, 1987).
5. Gerald Graff, *Professing Literature: An Institutional History* (Chicago: Univ. of Chicago Press, 1987), pp. 7–8.
6. Jon Pareles, "Sounds of Discord from Plato's Cave," *New York Times*, National Edition, 18 Oct. 1987, p. 30.

1. Crisis

1. John Henry Newman, "Knowledge Its Own End," in *The Idea of a University* (Garden City: Doubleday, 1959), p. 133.
2. *The Humanities in American Life* (Berkeley: Univ. of California Press, 1980), p. 66.
3. Helene Moglen, "Erosion in the Humanities: Blowing the Dust from Our Eyes," *Profession 83* (1983), p. 1.
4. Charles Newman, *The Post-Modern Aura: The Act of Fiction in an Age of Inflation* (Evanston, Ill.: Northwestern Univ. Press, 1985), p. 10.
5. Lionel Trilling, "The Meaning of a Literary Idea," in *The Liberal Imagination* (1950; rpt. Garden City, N.Y.: Doubleday, 1953), p. 277.
6. See, for example, the comments of William J. Bennett, "Endowment Chief Assails State of the Humanities on College Campuses," *Chronicle of Higher Education*, 28 Nov. 1984, pp. 1, 16–21; a report of the National Institute on Education, "U.S.

Colleges Not Realizing Their Full Potential," *Chronicle of Higher Education*, 24 Oct. 1984, pp. 1, 34–49; or a report of the American Association of Colleges, "Panel Calls Bachelor's Degree Meaningless," *Chronicle of Higher Education*, 13 Feb. 1985, pp. 1, 13–30.

7. Edward B. Fiske, "Commission on Education Warns 'Tide of Mediocrity' Imperils U.S.," *New York Times*, National Edition, p. 1.
8. "A Nation Prepared: Teachers for the 21st Century. Excerpts from the report by the Carnegie Forum's Task Force on Teaching as a Profession," *Chronicle of Higher Education*, 21 May 1986, p. 43.
9. Landon Y. Jones, *Great Expectations: America and the Baby Boom Generation* (New York: Ballantine, 1980), p. 180.
10. Dorothy K. Bestor, *Aside from Teaching, What in the World Can You Do? Career Strategies for Liberal Arts Graduates*, 2d ed. (Seattle: Univ. of Washington Press, 1982), p. 251.
11. See Richard B. Freeman, *The Over-Educated American* (New York: Academic Press, 1976), esp. chaps. 1 and 3.
12. Neal Woodruff, "Only Connect," *Profession 77* (1977), p. 57.
13. See, for example, the figures reported by the Modern Language Association, "PhD Survey," *MLA Newsletter* (Summer 1986), p. 14. The average tenure-track employment rate for 1983–84 is 38% for holders of Ph.D's in the languages, 36% for English.
14. Matthew Arnold, "The Function of Criticism at the Present Time," in *Poetry and Criticism of Matthew Arnold*, ed. A. Dwight Culler (Boston: Houghton Mifflin, 1961), p. 246.
15. William J. Bennett, " 'To Reclaim a Legacy': Text of Report on Humanities in Education," *Chronicle of Higher Education*, 28 Nov. 1984, p. 17.
16. Edward Said, "Opponents, Audiences, Constituencies, and Community," *Critical Inquiry* 9 (Sept. 1982): 22.

2. Work

1. John Naisbitt, *Megatrends: Ten New Directions Transforming Our Lives* (New York: Warner Books, 1982), p. 249.
2. *The Humanities in American Life* (Berkeley: Univ. of California Press, 1980), pp. 69–70.
3. David Lodge, *Small World* (New York: Macmillan, 1984), p. 28.
4. *A Guide for Job Candidates and Department Chairmen in English and Foreign Languages* (New York: Modern Language Association, 1975), p. 27.
5. "Notes on Publishing, Library Trends, and Research in the Humanities," *Scholarly Communication* 5 (Summer 1986): 4.
6. Denis Donoghue, *Ferocious Alphabets* (New York: Columbia Univ. Press, 1981), p. 51.
7. See, for example, Howard R. Bowen and Jack H. Schuster, "Outlook for the Academic Profession," *Academe*, September–October 1985, pp. 9–15. They estimate that as many as half a million new faculty appointments may be available in the next twenty-five years (p. 12).
8. For a discussion of the relative positions of Albert Shanker and Mary Hatwood Futrell, see Robert L. Jacobson, "NEA Backs Written Tests to Certify New Schoolteachers," *Chronicle of Higher Education*, 10 July 1985, p. 2.
9. Albert Shanker, "Where We Stand: Literacy Requires Learning the Culture," *New York Times*, National Edition, 4 Aug. 1985, p. E7.
10. William J. Bennett, " 'To Reclaim a Legacy': Text of Report on Humanities in Education." *Chronicle of Higher Education*, 28 Nov. 1984, p. 17.
11. For a discussion of the perhaps justifiable fears of the middle class, see Barbara

Ehrenreich, "Is the Middle Class Doomed," *New York Times Magazine*, 7 Sept. 1986, pp. 44ff.

12. "Freshman Characteristics and Attitudes," *Chronicle of Higher Education*, 16 Jan. 1985, pp. 15, 16.
13. "College Students: Who They Are, What They Think," *Chronicle of Higher Education*, 5 Feb. 1986, pp. 27, 29.
14. For a report of Kean's findings, see Scott Jaschik, "Project Will Aid States on College Reforms," *Chronicle of Higher Education*, 31 July 1985, p. 3.
15. See Scott Jaschik, "Governors Weigh Role of the States in Reform Efforts," *Chronicle of Higher Education*, 7 Aug. 1985, p. 14.
16. "Summary of 'Time for Results,' Report on Education by Governors' Group," *Chronicle of Higher Education*, 3 Sept. 1986, p. 78.
17. "Plans for Rating Colleges Sought," *New York Times*, National Edition, 29 Oct. 1985, p. 13.
18. "Summary of 'Time for Results,' " p. 79.
19. Donald Gray, "Another Year with College English," *College English* 44 (April 1982): 385.
20. Hazard S. Adams, "How Departments Commit Suicide," *Profession 83* (1983), p. 31.
21. Robert Lyons, "Mina Shaughnessy," in *Traditions of Inquiry*, ed. John Brereton (New York: Oxford Univ. Press, 1985), p. 174.
22. Paul Fussell, *Class: A Guide through the American Status System* (New York: Summit Books, 1983), p. 48.
23. See Pierre Bourdieu's discussion of "symbolic capital" in *Outline of a Theory of Practice*, trans. Richard Price, Cambridge Studies in Social Anthropology, No. 16 (Cambridge: Cambridge Univ. Press, 1977), pp. 171–83.
24. "Americans Give Their Schools High Marks in Poll," *Detroit Free Press*, 11 Aug. 1985, p. 6B.
25. John Herbers, "Governors Asking Greater Control over the Schools," *New York Times*, National Edition, 24 Aug. 1986, p. 1.
26. Gene I. Maeroff, "Alternate Route Leads Teachers to the Classroom," *New York Times*, National Edition, 13 Aug. 1985, p. 23.
27. For a report of the Carnegie Forum's findings, see "A Nation Prepared: Teachers for the 21st Century," *Chronicle of Higher Education*, 21 May 1986, pp. 43–54. For a report of the Holmes Group's findings, see "Test of Education-School Deans' Report on Reforms in Teacher Training," *Chronicle of Higher Education*, 9 Apr. 1986, pp. 27–37.
28. Robert L. Jacobson, "School-Reform Plan Could Cost as Much as $50-Billion," *Chronicle of Higher Education*, 28 May 1986, p. 23.
29. The best general study of part-time employment in the humanities is *Part-Time Academic Employment in the Humanities*, ed. M. Elizabeth Wallace (New York: Modern Language Association, 1984).
30. Robert von Hallberg, "Editor's Introduction," *Critical Inquiry* 10 (Sept. 1983): iii.
31. Edward W. Said, "Opponents, Audiences, Constituencies, and Community," *Critical Inquiry* 9 (Sept. 1982): p. 22.

3. History

1. John Stuart Mill, *Letters*, ed. H. S. R. Elliott, 2 vols. (London: Longmans, 1910), 2:359.
2. Matthew Arnold, *Poetry and Criticism of Matthew Arnold*, ed. A. Dwight Culler (Boston: Houghton Mifflin, 1961), p. 443. All subsequent quotations of Arnold's work are from this volume, with page citations included in the text.

3. George Eliot, *The Mill on the Floss*, ed. Gordon S. Haight (Boston: Houghton Mifflin, 1961), p. 64.
4. Thomas Henry Huxley, "A Liberal Education; and Where to Find It," in *English Prose of the Victorian Era*, ed. Charles Frederick Harrold and William D. Templeman (New York: Oxford Univ. Press, 1938), p. 1327.
5. Charles Dickens, *Great Expectations*, ed. Angus Calder (Harmondsworth: Penguin, 1981), p. 357.
6. G. Kitson Clark, *The Making of Victorian England* (1962; rpt. New York: Atheneum, 1974), p. 255.
7. See G. D. H. Cole and Raymond Postage, *The Common People, 1746–1946* (1938: rpt. London: Methuen, 1961), p. 128; and B. R. Mitchell and Phyllis Deane, *Abstract of British Historical Statistics* (Cambridge: Cambridge Univ. Press, 1962), p. 60. It should be noted that the English public schools, as well as the army, also offered the promise of culture and gentility. But neither played so instrumental a role in the representation of middle-class interests as did the university.
8. See, for example, Richard B. Freeman, *The Over-Educated American* (New York: Academic Press, 1976), pp. 33–50.
9. Thackeray's statement is quoted in W. L. Burn, *The Age of Equipoise: A Study of the Mid-Victorian Generation* (New York: Norton, 1965), p. 315.
10. Gerald Graff, *Literature against Itself: Literary Ideas in Modern Society* (Chicago: Univ. of Chicago Press, 1979), p. 92.
11. Janet L. Norwood, "The Growth in Service Jobs," *New York Times* National Edition, 28 Aug. 1985, p. 28.
12. See Martin J. Finkelstein, *The American Academic Profession: A Synthesis of Social Scientific Inquiry since World War II* (Columbus: Ohio State Univ. Press, 1984), pp. 7–31, 43–85.
13. "Change in America," *Chronicle of Higher Education*, 17 Sept. 1986, p. 1.
14. "Integrity in the College Curriculum," *Chronicle of Higher Education*, 13 Feb. 1985, p. 12.

4. Language

1. John Henry Newman, *The Idea of a University* (Garden City, N.Y.: Doubleday, 1959), p. 134.
2. "Department of English Tenure and Promotion Factors," Wayne State University English Department, 12 Nov. 1985, p. 4.
3. "Faculty Attitudes on Social and Educational Issues," *Chronicle of Higher Education*, 18 Dec.1985, p. 27.
4. "Two-Thirds of Public Says College Is 'Very Important,' " *Chronicle of Higher Education*, 25 Sept. 1985, p. 3.
5. "Summary of 'Time for Results,' Report on Education by Governors' Group," *Chronicle of Higher Education*, 3 Sept. 1986, p. 78.
6. "Plans for Rating Colleges Sought," *New York Times*, National Edition, 29 Oct. 1985, p. 13.
7. *Wayne State University Bulletin 1984–86* (Detroit: Wayne State Univ., 1984), p. 6.
8. Thomas Henry Huxley, "A Liberal Education; and Where to Find It," in *English Prose of the Victorian Period*, ed. Charles Frederick Harrold and William D. Templeman (New York: Oxford Univ. Press, 1938), p. 1327.
9. "Faculty Attitudes on Social and Educational Issues," *Chronicle of Higher Education*, 18 Dec. 1985, p. 26.
10. William Dean Howells, *Selected Letters*, ed. Robert C. Leitz III, Richard H. Ballinger, and Christoph K. Lohmann (Boston: Twayne Publishers, 1980), 3:45.

11. Matthew Arnold, *Poetry and Criticism of Matthew Arnold*, ed. A. Dwight Culler (Boston: Houghton Mifflin, 1961), p. 394.
12. Roger Shattuck, "How to Save Literature," *New York Review of Books*, 17 April 1980, pp. 29–35.
13. Michael Warner, "Professionalization and the Rewards of Literature: 1875–1900," *Criticism* 27 (Winter 1985): 21.
14. Raymond Federman, "Literary Theory in the University: A Survey," *New Literary History* 14 (Winter 1983): 417–18.
15. William J. Bennett, "Text of Secretary Bennett's Address Last Week at a Harvard University Anniversary Celebration," *Chronicle of Higher Education*, 15 Oct. 1986, p. 27.
16. Milan Kundera, *The Unbearable Lightness of Being*, trans. Michael Henry Heim (New York: Harper & Row, 1984).
17. For recent figures on the relation of academic salaries to inflation, see "Faculty Pay and the Cost of Living," *Chronicle of Higher Education*, 30 July 1986, p. 24.
18. Kundera, p. 5.
19. Walter Pater, "Style," in *English Prose of the Victorian Era*, ed. Charles Frederick Harrold and William D. Templeman (New York: Oxford Univ. Press, 1938), p. 1436.
20. William Strunk, Jr., and E. B. White, *The Elements of Style* (1959; rpt. New York: Macmillan, 1979), p. 70.
21. Fredric Jameson, *Marxism and Form: Twentieth-Century Dialectical Theories of Literature* (Princeton: Princeton Univ. Press, 1974), p. xii.
22. Bret Easton Ellis, "Down and Out at Bennington College," *Rolling Stone*, 26 Sept. 1985, p. 78.
23. Bret Easton Ellis, *Less Than Zero* (New York: Simon & Schuster, 1985), pp. 195–96.

5. Teachers and Students

1. [George Eliot], "Address to Working Men, By Felix Holt," in *Essays of George Eliot*, ed. Thomas Pinney (New York: Columbia Univ. Press, 1963), p. 425.
2. Gerald Graff, *Literature against Itself: Literary Ideas in Modern Society* (Chicago: Univ. of Chicago Press, 1979), p. 7.
3. William J. Bennett, " 'To Reclaim a Legacy': Text of Report on Humanities in Education," *Chronicle of Higher Education*, 28 Nov. 1984, pp. 17–18.
4. Walter Pater, *The Renaissance: Studies in Art and Poetry* (New York: New American Library, 1959), p. 157.
5. Jacques Derrida, *Of Grammatology*, trans. Gayatri Chakravorty Spivak (Baltimore: Johns Hopkins Univ. Press, 1976), pp. 158–59.
6. Landon Y. Jones, *Great Expectations: America and the Baby Boom Generation* (New York: Ballantine Books, 1980), p. 358.
7. Martin J. Finkelstein, *The American Academic Profession: A Synthesis of Social Scientific Inquiry since World War II* (Columbus: Ohio State Univ. Press, 1984), p. 33.
8. Oscar Wilde, "The Decay of Lying," in *Critical Theory since Plato*, ed. Hazard Adams (New York: Harcourt Brace Jovanovich, 1971), pp. 672–86.
9. Robert L. Jacobson, "Nearly 40 Pct. of Faculty Members Said to Consider Leaving Academe," *Chronicle of Higher Education*, 23 Oct. 1985, p. 1.
10. "A Nation Prepared: Teachers for the 21st Century," *Chronicle of Higher Education*, 21 May 1986, p. 44.
11. See, for example, Barbara Ehrenreich, "Is the Middle Class Doomed?" *New York Times Magazine*, 7 Sept. 1986, pp. 44, 50, 54, 62, 64; or Stephen Koepp, "Is the Middle Class Shrinking?" *Time*, 3 Nov. 1986, pp. 54–56.

12. Leslie Maitland Werner, "U.S. Literacy Survey Shows Mixed Results," *New York Times*, National Edition, 25 Sept. 1986, p. 1.
13. Lamar Alexander, "Summary of 'Time for Results,' Report on Education by Governors' Group," *Chronicle of High Education*, 3 Sept. 1986, p. 78.
14. "Plans for Rating Colleges Sought," *New York Times*, National Edition, 29 Oct. 1985, p. 13.
15. Hans Magnus Enzensberger, "In Praise of Illiteracy," *Harper's Magazine*, October 1986, p. 14.
16. Werner, p. 11.
17. Tzvetan Todorov, *The Conquest of America*, trans. Richard Howard (New York: Harper & Row, 1984), p. 252.
18. Jean Evangelauf, "National Reports on Undergraduate Education Spur Changes at 1 in 3 Colleges, Survey Finds," *Chronicle of Higher Education*, 30 July 1986, p. 20.
19. "Integrity in the College Curriculum," *Chronicle of Higher Education*, 13 Feb. 1985, p. 12.
20. Evangelauf, p. 20.
21. Scott Heller, "Extensive Use of Temporary Teachers Is Crippling Academe, AAUP Charges," *Chronicle of Higher Education*, 30 July 1986, p. 26.
22. Elaine El-Khawas, *Campus Trends, 1985* (Washington, D.C.: American Council on Education, 1986), combined figures for part-time and non-tenure hires, table 6, p. 11.
23. See Fredric Jameson, "Postmodernism, or the Cultural Logic of Late Capitalism," *New Left Review* 146 (July–August 1984), p. 72.
24. *What Works: Research about Teaching and Learning* (Washington, D.C.: U.S. Dept. of Education, 1986), p. iii.
25. All quotations are from a flyer titled "Building on Success with a New Edition of a Ground-Breaking Text," published by Scott, Foresman & Company of Glenview, Ill., in 1985. The flyer advertises new editions of two books by Elizabeth Cowan Neeld, *Writing* and *Writing: Brief* [pp. 1–10].
26. Ehrenreich, p. 44.

6. Subjects

1. Louis Harris, *Inside America* (New York: Vintage Books, 1987), p. 355.
2. Allan Bloom, *The Closing of the American Mind: How Higher Education Has Failed Democracy and Impoverished the Souls of Today's Students* (New York: Simon & Schuster, 1987); and E. D. Hirsch, Jr., *Cultural Literacy: What Every American Needs to Know* (Boston: Houghton Mifflin, 1987).

Conclusion

1. Henry T. Giroux, "Liberal Arts, Teaching, and Critical Literacy: Toward a Definition of Schooling as a Form of Cultural Politics," *Perspectives* 17 (Summer 1987), p. 23.
2. Raymond Williams, *Culture and Society, 1780–1950* (1958; rpt. New York: Harper & Row, 1966), p. 304.
3. See, in particular, the conclusion of Graff's *Professing Literature*.